Crock Pot Cookbook

Delicious and Lip-smacking Crock Pot Recipes

Michael Elliott

Crock-Pot Recipes for Dinner

Crock-Pot Chicken Recipes

Crock-Pot Meat Recipes

Crock-Pot Vegetable Recipes

Crock-Pot Soup Recipes

Crock-Pot Dessert Recipes

Introduction

Using slow cooker aka crockpot is a great way to save time and prepare nutritional meals. Just assemble meals in the morning and put in your crockpot. In the evening, your dinner will be ready without the excessive mess. This device requires a little amount of electricity to cook food as compared to another oven. While cooking, the slow cooker will not heat up your entire kitchen. Cooking with crockpot can be an economical choice because you can get the advantage of cheaper cuts of meat. The condensation acts as a self-baster and quickly tender tougher cuts in the crockpot. Therefore, while using a crockpot, you are saving time and money. Vegetables cooked in a crockpot can absorb spices and stocks and give them fuller flavors.

The low and high settings on crockpot allow you to adjust the temperature for the duration of cooking. Cooking on low is entirely safe, and if you are at home during the cooking process, you can cook on high setting for one hour to ensure through the cooking of food. Meat is a popular food to cook in the crockpot, but you should thaw frozen meat before, and they will take a long time to cook. You can heat meat to 140 °F to kill the bacteria in meat. Always ensure the internal temperature of meat within the recommended instructions before serving. While cooking poultry, use poultry with skin, and this will keep the meat moist during cooking procedure.

Preparation of vegetables in crockpot may take longer than meat, and it is essential to cut vegetables uniformly to cook them equally. If you are preparing stews or other vegetable dishes with meat, make sure to keep vegetables on the base of crockpot. Some slow cooker stews and soups require simmering for a longer period, and you can use low setting of the crockpot to cook these meals. Cover ingredients of soup with water, and you can add more liquid during cooking as per your needs. Spreads and dips are good to cook in crockpot on low setting with cheese. You can choose the warm setting or low heat to prepare dips without burning ingredients.

For a hot and nutritional breakfast, you can cook cracked wheat, rice porridge, and oatmeal overnight. Bread-based and bread dishes can be baked in a crockpot. The lower heating will help you to rise dough of bread. Another surprising category is dessert because tapioca and rice puddings are seemed to be a no-brainer, and you can use a crockpot to make cakes and fruit desserts. Some recipes require you to add ingredients near cooking time because of the nature of these ingredients. Herbs and spices may become too concentrated during cooking.

Make sure to adjust the levels of herbs and spices at the finishing point of cooking. Some dairy, seafood and vegetable products may lose their texture and flavor with long simmering. You should carefully follow the instructions in a recipe to avoid overcooking of ingredients. In this cookbook, you will find authentic crockpot recipes to cook nutritional meals.

Crock-Pot Recipes for Breakfast

1. Crock-Pot Moist Pancakes

(Time: 60 minutes \ Servings: 3)

Ingredients

2 eggs, whisked

½ cup milk

1 cup all-purpose flour

¼ teaspoon baking powder

1 pinch salt

¼ cup caster sugar

3-4 tablespoons honey

1 pinch baking soda

2 tablespoons butter

Some strawberry slices

Directions

In a bowl add butter and sugar, beat for 1-2 minutes or till smooth.

Now add eggs and beat continuously.

Add the sugar, milk, flour, baking powder, baking soda, salt, and beat for 1-2 minutes till a smooth batter is formed.

Spray crock-pot with cooking oil and transfer batter into pot and cover.

Set on high for 60 minutes.

Transfer the cake into a platter and top with honey.

Place some strawberry slices on top of the cake and serve.

2. Cinnamon Apple Canapé

(Time: 120 minutes \ Servings: 2)

Ingredients

1 egg, whisked

½ cup milk

4 tablespoons all-purpose flour

2 teaspoons caster sugar

3 tablespoons maple syrup

2 tablespoons butter, melted

¼ teaspoon cinnamon powder

3 large apples, peeled, thinly sliced

Directions

Take a bowl and combine egg, milk, flour, and sugar, mix to combine.

Grease crock-pot with butter and spread apple slices in pot.

Pour flour mixture over apples and sprinkle cinnamon powder on top.

Cover the crock-pot and set on high, cook for 120 minutes.

Transfer to a serving dish and drizzle maple syrup. Enjoy.

3. Cheesy Potato Tortilla

(Time: 60 minutes \ Servings: 3)

Ingredients

4 eggs, whisked

2 small potatoes, thinly sliced

½ cup mozzarella cheese, grated

½ teaspoon salt

½ teaspoon black pepper

2 tablespoons butter

Directions

Beat eggs in a medium bowl till creamy.

Add in mozzarella cheese, cream cheese, salt, pepper, and potatoes, mix well.

Grease the crock-pot. Cover the crock-pot with lid and set on high, cook for 60 minutes.

Transfer to a serving platter and serve hot. Enjoy.

4. Creamy Turkey Casserole

(Time: 120 minutes \ Servings: 4)

Ingredients

1 skim milk

1 cup turkey, boiled, shredded

1 cup mozzarella cheese, grated

1 cup parmesan cheese, grated

¼ teaspoon salt

1 small onion, chopped

¼ teaspoon garlic powder

2 tablespoons butter, melted

Directions

Add butter, onion, turkey and garlic powder in crock pot and stir.

Now transfer the mozzarella cheese, parmesan cheese, and milk, and stir.

Cover the crock pot with lid and cook for 2 hours. Serve and enjoy.

5. Spinach Omelette

(Time: 60 minutes \ Servings: 2)

Ingredients

2 eggs, whisked

½ cup baby spinach leaves

¼ teaspoon salt

1 pinch black pepper

1 tablespoon butter, melted

Directions

In a medium bowl add the eggs, salt, pepper and mix to combine.

Add butter into the crock-pot and transfer the eggs mixture into the pot.

Place spinach leaves on top and cover the pot with lid, cook on high for 60 minutes.

Transfer to a serving platter and serve hot.

Enjoy.

6. Chickpea and Spinach Pie

(Time: 120 minutes \ Servings: 4)

Ingredients

2 cup chickpea, boiled

3 eggs, whisked

1 cup baby spinach leaves

¼ teaspoon salt

½ black pepper

¼ cup parmesan cheese, grated

2 tablespoons butter, melted

Directions

Transfer the eggs, chickpea, spinach, cheese, and butter into crock-pot, stir well.

Season with salt and pepper. Cover the crock-pot with lid and leave to cook on high T for 2 hours. Transfer to a serving dish. Serve and enjoy.

7. Tuna Tartlet

(Time: 60 minutes \ Servings: 2)

Ingredients

3 oz. tuna pieces

2 eggs, whisked

¼ teaspoon salt

¼ chili powder

1 tablespoon cooking oil

Kiwi for garnishing, chopped and sliced

Directions

Spray the crock-pot with oil and transfer the eggs, tuna. Combine well.

Season with salt and chili powder.

Cover crock-pot and let to prepare for 60 minutes.

Now transfer to serving dish and shred with folk.

Top with chopped kiwi as much you like.

Serve and enjoy.

8. Tomato and Egg Tart

(Time: 120 minutes \ Servings: 6)

Ingredients

3 eggs, whisked

2 potatoes, peeled, thinly sliced

1 tablespoon coriander leaves, chopped

1 onion, sliced

2 tomatoes, chopped

¼ teaspoon salt

½ chili powder

2 tablespoons butter, melted

Directions

Combine the eggs, onion, tomatoes, coriander, and potatoes, mix well.

Transfer to the crock-pot and sprinkle salt and chili powder on top.

Cover with lid and cook on high for 2 hours. Put to a serving dish. Serve and enjoy.

9. Crock-Pot Risotto

(Time: 120 minutes \ Servings: 4)

Ingredients

1 ½ cups Arborio rice

¼ cup dried tomatoes

1 egg, whisked

1 cup milk

¼ cup cream

2 cups chicken broth

¼ cup baby spinach leaves

¼ teaspoon salt

½ black pepper

2 tablespoons butter, melted

Directions

In the crock-pot, add butter, rice, tomatoes, and egg, stir to combine well.

Transfer the spinach, cream, milk, salt, pepper, and mix.

Pour in chicken broth and cover the crock-pot with lid.

Cook on high for 2 hours.

Put to a serving dish.

Serve hot and enjoy.

10. Banana and Quinoa Smash

(Time: 240 minutes \ Servings: 4)

Ingredients

2 cup quinoa

2 cups milk

¼ cup caster sugar

2 tablespoons honey

1 tablespoons brown sugar

1 cup cream

2 bananas

3 tablespoons butter, melted

Directions

Peel the bananas and mash with folk till smooth.

Transfer the milk, quinoa, sugar, butter, honey, brown sugar, and cream into crock-pot, mix well. Add in the bananas and stir to combine.

Cover the crock-pot with lid and cook on high for 3-4 hours. Transfer to a serving dish. Serve and enjoy.

11. Pumpkin Bread

(Time: 60 minutes \ Servings: 12)

Ingredients

1 cup pumpkin puree

2 cups all-purpose flour

3 eggs

1 cup milk

¼ baking powder

1 pinch baking soda

1 tablespoon yeast

¼ cup warm water

½ cup butter

Directions

Beat the eggs in a bowl till creamy.

In a separate bowl beat butter for 1 minute, now add sugar, beat again till smooth.

Combine the egg and butter mixture, add in milk, beat for 1-2 minutes.

In water, add yeast and let to sit for 5-10 minute.

Pour the pumpkin puree and yeast mixture into batter and mix well.

Now add baking soda, flour, and stir to combine. Transfer butter into bread mould and place it in the crock pot. Cover with lid and cook on high for 60 minutes.

After that remove mould and slice the bread. Transfer the bread slices to a serving platter.

Serve and enjoy.

12. Spinach and Potato Casserole

(Time: 120 minutes \ Servings: 4)

Ingredients

1 cup spinach, chopped

3 potatoes, peeled, shredded

1 onion, chopped

1 egg, whisked

2 oz. cream cheese, crumbled

2 tablespoons sugar

1 cup mozzarella cheese, shredded

¼ teaspoon salt

¼ teaspoon black pepper

Directions

In the crock-pot add spinach, potatoes, onion, egg, sugar, salt, pepper and toss to combine.

Now add the cream cheese and mozzarella cheese. Cover the crock-pot with lid and cook on high for 2hours. Transfer to serving dish and enjoy.

13. French Toast

(Time: 60 minutes \ Servings: 2)

Ingredients

2-4 bread slices

1 eggs

2 tablespoons caster sugar

2 tablespoons honey

1 cup milk

2 tablespoons butter

Directions

Turn on the crock-pot and add in butter. In a bowl crack egg and whisk for 2-3 minutes.

Add in sugar, milk and whisk again till sugar is dissolved.

Dip each bread slice into eggs mixture and transfer into the crock-pot.

Cover the crock-pot with lid and cook on high for 1 hour from one side, then flip the side and cook for another hour.

Transfer to a serving platter and drizzle honey on top. Serve and enjoy.

14. Egg and Bananas French Rolls

(Time: 60 minutes \ Servings: 4)

Ingredients

2-4 bread slices

2-4 bananas, peeled

2 eggs

2 tablespoons caster sugar

½ cup low fat milk

2 tablespoons butter, melted

3-4 tablespoons maple syrup

Directions

In a bowl add the eggs and whisk a little. Add the sugar and milk, whisk till sugar is dissolved.

Dip bread slices into eggs mixture and place a banana into each bread slice and roll out carefully, transfer into the crock-pot. Cover the crock-pot with lid and cook on high for 1 hour.

Transfer to a serving platter and drizzle maple syrupy. Serve and enjoy.

15. Tropical Chocolate Oatmeal

(Time: 120 minutes \ Servings: 4)

Ingredients

2 cups oatmeal

2 cups milk

1 banana, mashed

½ cup cocoa powder

½ cup cream

¼ cup caster sugar

¼ cup raw chocolate

2 tablespoons honey

4 tablespoons butter

Directions

Transfer the milk, oats, sugar, cocoa powder, cream, honey, banana, and chocolate into crock-pot, stir to combine.

Cover up with lid and cook on low for 2 hours. Serve hot and enjoy.

16. Moist French Toast Casserole

(Time: 60 minutes \ Servings: 3)

Ingredients

7-8 bread slices, roughly shredded

1 egg, whisked

3 tablespoons caster sugar

1 cup parmesan cheese, grated

3 cups milk

1 cup cream

3 tablespoons butter, melted

Directions

Combine the milk, butter, sugar, parmesan cheese, cream, and egg into medium bowl.

Put the bread pieces into the crock-pot and pour the milk mixture.

Cover the crock-pot with lid and cook on low for 1 hour. Serve and enjoy!

17. Raisin Bread Pudding

(Time: 120 minutes \ Servings: 3)

Ingredients

10-12 bread slices, roughly shredded

2 egg, whisked

¼ cup caster sugar

4 cups milk

1 cup raisins

4 tablespoons butter, melted

Directions

In the Crock Pot add all the ingredients and toss to combine.

Cover the crock-pot with lid and cook on high for 2 hours.

Put to a serving dish and enjoy.

18. Breakfast Granola Bowl

(Time: 180 minutes \ Servings: 4)

Ingredients

2 cups granola

½ cup brown sugar

4 cups milk

1 cup strawberries, sliced

2 tablespoons honey

½ cup cream, whipped

4 tablespoons butter, melted

Directions

Transfer the granola, brown sugar, honey, butter, and milk, stir to combine.

Put cover on the crock-pot and cook on low for 3 hours.

Transfer to a serving bowl and place some strawberries.

Top with puddle of whipped cream. Drizzle, serve and enjoy.

19. Crock-Pot Ricotta Oats

(Time: 180 minutes \ Servings: 2)

Ingredients

2 cups oats

½ cup rice, boiled

4 oz. ricotta cheese

2 cups milk

½ cup coconut milk

½ cup sugar

1 tablespoon coconut oil

Directions

Fill the crock-pot with oats, rice, coconut milk, ricotta cheese, milk, coconut oil, and sugar, stir to combine well.

Place lid over the crock-pot and set it to cook on low for 3 hours.

Put to a serving bowl. Serve and enjoy.

20. Oats and Banana Crumble

(Time: 120 minutes \ Servings: 3)

Ingredients

2 cups oats

1 egg, whisked

4 bananas, cut into 1 inch slices

¼ cup brown sugar

3 cups cream milk

2 tablespoons honey

2 tablespoons butter, melted

Directions

In the Crock Pot add the oats, egg, bananas, sugar, honey, milk, and butter, toss well to combine. Cover the crock-pot with lid and cook on high for 2 hours.

Transfer to a serving bowl. Serve and enjoy.

21. Baked Glazed Apple Mash

(Time: 120 minutes \ Servings: 2)

Ingredients

4-6 apples, peeled, cut into 1 inch slices

¼ cup caster sugar

2 tablespoons honey

1 cup apple juice

1 tablespoon lemon juice

2 tablespoons butter, melted

Directions

Fill your crock-pot with apples, sugar, honey, lemon juice, apple juice, and butter, mix well.

Cover up the crock-pot and cook on high for 2 hours.

Transfer to a serving dish.

Serve and enjoy.

22. Blueberry Cheese Casserole

(Time: 120 minutes \ Servings: 3)

Ingredients

1 cup blueberries

1 cup milk

¼ cup caster sugar

1 cup ricotta cheese, crumbled

½ cup cheddar cheese, crumbled

1 cup mozzarella cheese, grated

2 tablespoons butter, melted

Directions

In the Crock Pot add all ingredients and toss to combine well.

Cover the crock-pot with lid and cook on high for 2 hours.

Put to a serving dish. Serve and enjoy.

23. Strawberry Chia Bowl

(Time: 120 minutes \ Servings: 2)

Ingredients

2 cups chia seeds

1 egg, whisked

½ cup caster sugar

2 cups skim milk

½ cup almond milk

1 cup strawberries

4 tablespoons butter, melted

Directions

Put the chia seeds, egg, skim milk, almond milk, strawberries, and butter, mix well.

Place the cover over the crock-pot and set it on high for 2 hours.

When done, ladle into a serving bowl and top with your favorite fruits.

Serve hot and enjoy.

24. Pumpkin Bread Pudding

(Time: 180 minutes \ Servings: 4)

Ingredients

2 oz. bread, roughly shredded

1 cup pumpkin puree

½ teaspoon pumpkin spice

2 tablespoons sugar

2 cups cream milk

2 tablespoons butter

Directions

In the Crock Pot add all ingredients and toss to combine.

Cover the Crock-Pot with lid and cook on high for 3 hours.

Transfer to a serving dish. Serve immediately.

25. Quinoa and Oats Pudding

(Time: 120 minutes \ Servings: 2)

Ingredients

1 cup quinoa

1 cup oats

2 tablespoons brown sugar

4 tablespoon maple syrup

2 cups milk

3 tablespoons butter, melted

1 cup blackberries

Directions

In the Crock Pot add all ingredients and toss to combine.

Cover the crock-pot with lid and cook on high for 2 hours.

Put to a serving dish.

Serve and enjoy.

Crock-Pot Recipes for Lunch

26. Crock-Pot Spiced Chickpea

(Time: 420 minutes \ Servings: 8)

Ingredients

2 cups, chickpea, soaked overnight

4 cups chicken broth

2-3 garlic cloves, minced

1 teaspoon ginger paste

1 cup tomato sauce

1 onion, chopped

½ teaspoon salt

¼ teaspoon turmeric powder

½ teaspoon cinnamon powder

½ teaspoon cumin powder

½ teaspoon chili powder

2 cloves

1 bay leaf

2 tablespoons olive oil

Directions

Transfer the chickpea, chicken broth, bay leaf, cloves, tomato sauce, ginger, garlic, onion, salt, chili powder, cumin powder, cinnamon powder, turmeric powder, and oil into the crock pot, stir.

Cover with lid and let it cook for 7 hours on low.

Transfer to a serving dish.

Serve hot with rice or bread and enjoy.

27. Roasted Potatoes

(Time: 120 minutes \ Servings: 3)

Ingredients

4 potatoes, peeled, diced

1 teaspoon garlic powder

½ teaspoon salt

¼ teaspoon black pepper

¼ teaspoon cumin powder

½ teaspoon dried rosemary

¼ teaspoon chili powder

2 tablespoons lemon juice

¼ cup oil

Directions

In a bowl mix the garlic powder, oil, salt, black pepper, rosemary, cumin powder, chili powder, and lemon juice, toss to combine.

Transfer the potatoes into the crock-pot and pour oil over the potatoes, stir.

Cover with lid and let it cook for 2 hours on high. Serve with desired sauce and enjoy.

28. Crock-Pot Carrot and Peas Pilaf

(Time: 120 minutes \ Servings: 6)

Ingredients

1 cup rice, soaked for 30 minutes

2 cups chicken broth

2 carrots, chopped

1 cup peas

¼ cup fried onion

1 teaspoon salt

½ teaspoon cumin seeds

2-3 cinnamon sticks

½ teaspoon chili powder

3 tablespoons olive oil

Directions

Put the rice, chicken broth, carrots, peas and fried onion into the crock-pot and stir.

Add the salt, chili powder, cumin seeds, cinnamon sticks, and oil mix thoroughly.

Cover the pot with lid and cook for 2 hours on high.

Transfer to a serving platter. Serve hot and enjoy with desired salsa or salad.

29. Chickpea and Spinach Curry

(Time: 420 minutes \ Servings: 8)

Ingredients

1 cup, chickpea, soaked overnight

1 cup baby spinach, chopped

4 cups vegetable broth

1 teaspoon garlic paste

1 teaspoon ginger paste

2 tomatoes, chopped

¼ cup fried onion

1 teaspoon salt

¼ teaspoon turmeric powder

½ teaspoon chili powder

2 green chilies, chopped

3 tablespoons olive oil

1 tablespoon butter

Directions

Transfer the spinach, chickpea, vegetable broth, tomatoes, ginger garlic paste, onion, salt, chili powder, turmeric powder, and oil into crock pot, stir to combine.

Cover with lid and let it cook for 7 hours on low. Transfer to a serving dish and top with butter. Serve immediately and enjoy.

30. Crock-Pot Zucchini and Chickpea Stew

(Time: 420 minutes \ Servings: 6)

Ingredients

1 cup, chickpea, soaked overnight

1 zucchini, sliced

¼ cup cauliflower florets

2 carrots, chopped

3 cups vegetable broth

2-3 garlic cloves, minced

1 onion, chopped

1 tablespoons soya sauce

1 tablespoon vinegar

1 teaspoon salt

¼ teaspoon turmeric powder

½ teaspoon chili powder

2 tablespoons olive oil

Directions

In the Crock-Pot, add the chickpea, carrots, zucchini, cauliflower, vegetable broth, garlic, onion, salt, chili powder, turmeric powder, and oil, stir to combine.

Cover with lid and let it cook for 6-7 hours on low. Serve and enjoy.

31. Crock-Pot Whole Turkey

(Time: 240 minutes \ Servings: 6)

Ingredients

1 whole turkey	2 teaspoons salt
1 tablespoons garlic paste	¼ teaspoon turmeric powder
½ teaspoon ginger paste	1 teaspoon cayenne pepper
3 tablespoons soya sauce	½ teaspoon cumin powder
2 tablespoons vinegar	½ teaspoon cinnamon powder
¼ cup lemon juice	4 tablespoons olive oil

Directions

In a bowl add the ginger garlic paste, vinegar, olive oil, lemon juice, soya sauce, salt, cayenne pepper, and turmeric powder, mix well.

Pour over the turkey and rub all over. Let it sit for 30 minutes. Transfer to a greased crock-pot and place the lid on the pot. Cook for 3-4 hours on high. Serve and enjoy.

32. Hot Quinoa Chili

(Time: 300 minutes \ Servings: 4)

Ingredients

2 cups quinoa	1 tablespoon vinegar
1 cup tomato sauce	1 teaspoons salt
4 cups vegetable broth	1 teaspoon cayenne pepper
4 tablespoons chili garlic sauce	½ teaspoon cinnamon powder
2 tablespoons soya sauce	2 tablespoons olive oil

Directions

In the Crock-Pot add the quinoa, vegetable broth, tomato sauce, chili garlic paste, vinegar, olive oil, soya sauce, salt, cinnamon powder, and cayenne pepper, mix well.

Cover the crock-pot with a lid. Cook for 5-6 hours on low. Serve and enjoy.

33. Velvety Lentil Gravy

(Time: 300 minutes \ Servings: 6)

Ingredients

1 cup yellow lentil, soaked

1 cup red lentil, soaked

½ cup split gram, soaked

2 tomatoes, chopped

2 cups vegetable broth

2 cups hot water

1 teaspoon garlic paste

1 teaspoons salt

1 teaspoon cayenne pepper

¼ teaspoon turmeric powder

½ teaspoon cinnamon powder

½ cup sour cream

2 tablespoons olive oil

Directions

In the Crock-Pot add the yellow lentil, red lentil, split gram, tomatoes, water, vegetable broth, garlic paste, olive oil, turmeric powder, salt, cinnamon powder, and cayenne pepper, mix well.

Cover the crock-pot with a lid. Leave it cook for 5-6 hours on low. Top with sour cream.

34. Black Lentils Curry

(Time: 240 minutes \ Servings: 6)

Ingredients

2 cups black lentils, soaked for 2 hours

½ cup tomatoes puree

3 cups vegetable broth

1 teaspoon garlic paste

¼ teaspoon ginger paste

1 teaspoons salt

1 teaspoon black pepper

¼ teaspoon turmeric powder

½ teaspoon cinnamon powder

½ teaspoon cumin powder

½ cup sour cream

3 tbsp butter and 1 chopped coriander

Directions

In the crock-pot add the lentils, tomato puree, water, vegetable broth, ginger garlic paste, butter, turmeric powder, salt, cumin powder, cinnamon powder, and black pepper, mix to combine.

Cover the crock-pot with a lid.

Leave it cook for 3-4 hours on high.

Transfer to a serving bowl, top with sour cream and coriander.

Serve and enjoy.

35. Turkey Chili Curry

(Time: 120 minutes \ Servings: 4)

Ingredients

1 cup turkey, pieces

2 red bell pepper, sliced

2 yellow bell peppers, sliced

1 cup tomato puree

2 tablespoons vinegar

2 cups vegetable broth

1 teaspoon garlic paste

1 teaspoons salt

2 tablespoons fried onion

1 teaspoon cayenne pepper

¼ teaspoon turmeric powder

½ cup sour cream

2 tablespoons olive oil

1 tablespoon coriander, chopped

Directions

In the Crock-Pot add the turkey pieces, bell peppers, onion, vinegar, tomato puree, vegetable broth, garlic paste, olive oil, turmeric powder, salt, and cayenne pepper, mix well.

Cover with a lid.

Leave it cook for 2 hours on low.

Put to a serving bowl, top with sour cream and chopped coriander.

Serve and enjoy.

36. Creamy White Lentil and Corn

(Time: 240 minutes \ Servings: 4)

Ingredients

1 cup white beans, soaked

1 cup corn kernel

1 cup sour cream

½ cup coconut milk

2 tablespoons lemon juice

3 cups vegetable broth

1 teaspoon garlic paste

1 teaspoons salt

2 tablespoons butter

2 tablespoons tomato ketchup

1 tablespoon coriander, chopped

Directions

In the crock-pot add the white beans, coconut milk, sour cream, corn kernels, tomato ketchup, vegetable broth, garlic paste, butter, and salt, mix well.

Transfer to a crock-pot and cover with a lid, leave it cook for 4 hours on low.

Ladle to a serving bowl, sprinkle chopped coriander and drizzle lemon juice.

37. Quinoa and Peas Platter

(Time: 180 minutes \ Servings: 2)

Ingredients

1 cup quinoa

1 cup peas

3 cups vegetable broth

1 teaspoon garlic paste

1 teaspoons salt

2 tablespoons fried onion

¼ teaspoon chili powder

¼ teaspoon turmeric powder

2 tablespoons olive oil

Directions

Fill your Crock Pot with the quinoa, peas, turmeric powder, oil, vegetable broth, onion, garlic and mix to combine. Season with salt and chili powder.

Leave it cook for 3 hours on low. Put to a serving platter.

Serve and enjoy.

38. Sweet Potato Turkey Gravy

(Time: 120 minutes \ Servings: 4)

Ingredients

1 cup turkey, minced

3 sweet potatoes, peeled, diced

1 cup squash, grated

1 onion, sliced

½ cup green onions, chopped

2 green bell pepper, sliced

1 cup tomato puree

2 cups vegetable broth

1 teaspoon garlic paste

1 teaspoons salt

1 teaspoon cayenne pepper

¼ teaspoon turmeric powder

2 tablespoons olive oil

Directions

In the Crock-Pot add the turkey mince, bell pepper, onion, sweet potatoes, tomato puree, vegetable broth, garlic paste, olive oil, turmeric powder, salt, and cayenne pepper, stir to combine well.

Leave it cook for 2 hours on low. Put to a serving dish and sprinkle green onions. Serve and enjoy.

39. Crock-Pot Baked Potatoes and Carrots

(Time: 180 minutes \ Servings: 4)

Ingredients

4 potatoes, peeled, diced

4 carrots, diced

½ teaspoon garlic powder

1 tablespoon dried rosemary

1 teaspoon ginger paste

1 teaspoons salt

1 teaspoon black pepper

2 tablespoons olive oil

½ teaspoon cumin powder

¼ cup apple cider vinegar

Directions

Put the potatoes and carrots into the Crock-Pot.

Take a bowl and mix the vinegar, salt, cumin powder, pepper, rosemary, ginger paste, garlic powder, and oil, mix well. Pour over the potatoes and the carrots, toss to combine.

Leave it cook for 3 hours on high. Serve hot and enjoy.

40. Crock-Pot Loaded Potatoes

(Time: 240 minutes \ Servings: 2)

Ingredients

2 large potatoes, halved

1 cup sour cream

1 teaspoons salt

1 teaspoon cinnamon powder

2 tablespoon dill

2 tablespoons olive oil

Directions

Place the potatoes into the pot and cover up with a lid, cook on high for 4 hours.

Now scop out the flash of the potatoes and fill with sour cream. Sprinkle salt and cinnamon powder. Top with chopped dill, serve and enjoy.

41. Soya Brussels Sprouts

(Time: 300 minutes \ Servings: 6)

Ingredients

6 oz. Brussels sprouts

4 tablespoons soya sauce

1 teaspoons salt

2 tablespoons lemon juice

1 teaspoon black pepper

4 tablespoons olive oil

Directions

Place the sprouts into the Crock-Pot and drizzle soya sauce, lemon juice, and olive oil.

Season with salt and pepper, toss to combine.

Cover the Crock-Pot with a lid and let it prepare for 4 hours on high.

Put to a served dish.

Serve and enjoy.

42. Steamed Ginger Shrimps

(Time: 120 minutes \ Servings: 4)

Ingredients

4 oz. shrimps

1 teaspoon ginger paste

1 teaspoons salt

½ teaspoon chili powder

2 tablespoon lemon juice

1 tablespoon soya sauce

¼ cup apple cider vinegar

2 tablespoons olive oil

Directions

Toss the shrimps with olive oil, ginger paste, vinegar, salt, chili powder, lemon juice and soya sauce. Transfer to a deep baking dish that can be placed into the Crock-Pot.

Add 2 cups of water into the crock-pot and place a baking dish into the pot, cover with a lid.

Let it prepare on high for 2 hours. Serve and enjoy.

43. Crock-Pot Steamed Tomato Fish

(Time: 120 minutes \ Servings: 2)

Ingredients

2 fish fillets

1 teaspoon garlic paste

1 teaspoons salt

2 tomatoes, sliced

½ teaspoon chili powder

2 tablespoons vinegar

2 tablespoons olive oil

Directions

Transfer the fish and the tomatoes into a deep baking dish that can be fitted into the crock-pot. Combine the olive oil, garlic paste, vinegar, salt, and chili powder.

Pour over the fish and the tomatoes.

Add 2 cups of water into the crock-pot and place the baking dish into the pot, cover with a lid. Leave it cook on high for 2 hours. Transfer to a serving dish.

Serve and enjoy.

44. Creamy Fish Mac

(Time: 120 minutes \ Servings: 3)

Ingredients

2 fish fillets, pieces

2 yellow bell peppers, sliced

1 leak, sliced

1 cup heavy cream

1 cup parmesan cheese, grated

1 teaspoon garlic paste

1 teaspoons salt

½ teaspoon black pepper

1 package macaroni

2 tablespoons vinegar

2 cups vegetable broth

2 tablespoons olive oil

Directions

Transfer the fish with cream, vegetable broth, cheese, pepper, bell pepper, leak, olive oil, garlic paste, vinegar, and salt. Stir to combine and cover with a lid.

Leave it cook on high for 2 hours. Serve and enjoy.

45. Crock-Pot Veggie Noodle Stew

(Time: 120 minutes \ Servings: 2)

Ingredients

2 carrots, shredded

1 package noodles

2 cups chicken stock

1 onion, sliced

1 cup cabbage, chopped

½ cup kale leaves, roughly chopped

1 zucchini, spiralized

2 tablespoons soya sauce

1 teaspoon garlic paste

1 teaspoons salt

2 tablespoons vinegar

2 tablespoons olive oil

Directions

Transfer all the ingredients into the crock-pot and cover up with a lid.

Leave it cook on high for 2 hours on high.

Serve and enjoy.

46. Crock-Pot Tuna Pasta

(Time: 120 minutes \ Servings: 4)

Ingredients

2 oz. tuna, pieces

1 package pasta

2 cups chicken stock

1 teaspoon garlic paste

1 teaspoons salt

¼ cup green onion, chopped

1 cup sour cream

2 tablespoons olive oil

Directions

Transfer all the ingredients into the Crock-Pot and cove up with a lid.

Let it cook on high for 2 hours on high.

Put to a serving dish and enjoy.

47. Crock-Pot Tomato Corn Stew

(Time: 180 minutes \ Servings: 4)

Ingredients

4 tomatoes, sliced

2 carrots, sliced

1 onion, sliced

1 cup corn kernels

3 cups vegetable broth

1 cup hot water

2 garlic cloves, minced

1 teaspoons salt

¼ teaspoon chili powder

2 tablespoons olive oil

Directions

In the Crock-Pot add the tomatoes, onion, carrots, oil, corn kernels, water, garlic, vegetable broth, salt, chili powder, and cove up with a lid.

Let it cook on high for 3 hours on high.

Ladle to a serving dish.

Serve hot and enjoy.

48. Red Lentil Masala

(Time: 120 minutes \ Servings: 4)

Ingredients

1 cup red lentil, soaked

2 cups chicken stock

1 teaspoon garlic paste

1 teaspoons salt

1 teaspoon cayenne pepper

2 tablespoons olive oil

1 cup tomato paste

1 teaspoon cumin seeds

1 teaspoon ginger paste

1 tablespoon coriander, chopped

Directions

Fill the Crock-Pot with a lentil, tomato paste, pepper, cumin seeds, ginger garlic paste, chicken stock, oil, and salt, cover up with a lid.

Let it cook on high for 2 hours on high.

Put to a serving dish and top with coriander. Serve and enjoy.

49. Crock-Pot Shrimps Curry

(Time: 120 minutes \ Servings: 4)

Ingredients

4 oz. shrimps

2 cups chicken stock

1 teaspoon garlic paste

1 teaspoons salt

¼ teaspoon cayenne pepper

2 tablespoons olive oil

1 cup yogurt

¼ teaspoon turmeric powder

1 tablespoon coriander, chopped

1 bay leaf

1 tablespoon coriander, chopped

Directions

Fill the Crock-Pot with shrimps, chicken stock, yogurt, turmeric powder, coriander, bay leaf, pepper, garlic paste, oil, and salt, stir and cover the pot with a lid.

Cook on high for 2 hours on high.

Ladle to a serving dish and serve.

Enjoy.

50. Traditional Saffron Rice

(Time: 120 minutes \ Servings: 4)

Ingredients

1 cup rice, soaked

1 pinch saffron

1 cup hot water

1 teaspoons salt

4 tablespoons olive oil

¼ cup fried onion

2 cups chicken broth

Directions

In a cup add water and saffron, stir to combine.

Now add the rice, chicken broth, salt, oil, onion, and saffron mixture, into crock-pot, mix well.

Let it cook on high for 2 hours on high.

Serve and enjoy.

Crock-Pot Recipes for Dinner

51. Crock-Pot Cheesy Macaroni

(Time: 120 minutes \ Servings: 3)

Ingredients

1 package macaroni

1 teaspoon garlic powder

2 oz. mozzarella cheese

2 oz. parmesan cheese

2 cups hot chicken broth

½ teaspoon salt

¼ teaspoon cinnamon powder

2 tablespoons olive oil

Directions

Combine the mozzarella cheese and the parmesan cheese into a bowl and crumble with a fork.

Transfer the macaroni, chicken broth, salt, garlic powder, oil, and cheese mixture into crock-pot, stir well.

Cover the pot with a lid and let it cook for 2 hours on high.

Transfer to a serving dish and sprinkle cinnamon powder.

Serve hot and enjoy.

52. Creamy Wild Rice with Tofu

(Time: 180 minutes \ Servings: 3)

Ingredients

1 cup wild rice

1 cup sour cream

1 cup ricotta cheese

3 oz. tofu

1 teaspoon garlic powder

2 oz. ricotta cheese

2 carrots, peeled, sliced

1 can chicken soup

2 cups hot chicken broth

½ teaspoon sea salt

1 teaspoon cumin seeds

Directions

Pour the chicken broth, sour cream, and chicken soup into the crock pot.

Add in the ricotta cheese, tofu, carrots, garlic powder, sea salt, cumin seeds and rice, mix all ingredients well. Cover the pot with a lid and let it cook for 2 hours on high.

Transfer to a serving dish and enjoy.

53. Crock-Pot Cheesy Corn

(Time: 300 minutes \ Servings: 3)

Ingredients

2 cups corn kernels

4 cups hot water

2 oz. mozzarella cheese

2 oz. parmesan cheese

½ teaspoon salt

Directions

In the Crock-Pot add corn kernels, water and salt, let it cook on high for 4 hours.

Now add the parmesan cheese and mix well, cover and cook again for 1 hour.

Transfer to a serving dish.

Serve immediately and enjoy.

54. Crock-Pot Steamed Maple Salmon

(Time: 120 minutes \ Servings: 2)

Ingredients

2 fish fillets

1 teaspoon garlic powder

4 tablespoon maple syrup

2 tablespoon vinegar

1 tablespoon lemon juice

2 tablespoon soya sauce

½ teaspoon salt

½ teaspoon white powder

2 tablespoons olive oil

2 tablespoon coriander, chopped

Directions

In a bowl add the vinegar, olive oil, lemon juice, maple syrup, soya sauce, white pepper, salt, and garlic powder, mix well.

Pour this mixture over the salmon and rub all over. Transfer into a deep baking dish.

Place a baking dish into the crock pot and cover up with a lid. Cook for 2 hours.

Transfer into a platter and sprinkle chopped coriander. Serve hot and enjoy.

55. Crock-Pot Corn and Black Beans

(Time: 300 minutes \ Servings: 3)

Ingredients

1 cup black beans, soaked

1 cup quinoa

1 cup corn kernels

1 teaspoon garlic powder

4 cups hot water

1 onion, sliced

1 teaspoon kosher salt

2 tablespoons olive oil

Directions

Put the water, quinoa, black beans, kernels, quinoa, salt, onion, and oil into crock-pot, mix thoroughly.

Cover and let it cook for 5 hours on low. Now transfer to a serving dish.

Serve and enjoy.

56. Crock-Pot Black Bean Curry

(Time: 300 minutes \ Servings: 3)

Ingredients

1 ½ cup black beans, soaked

1 teaspoon garlic powder

1 onion, chopped

2 tomatoes, chopped

1 cup chicken broth

½ teaspoon ginger paste

4 cups hot water

1 teaspoon kosher salt

½ teaspoon black pepper

2 tablespoons olive oil

Directions

In the Crock Pot add all ingredients and toss well to combine thoroughly.

Cover the pot and let it cook for 5 hours on low. Now transfer to a serving dish and enjoy.

57. Crock-Pot Lentils and Squash Curry

(Time: 300 minutes \ Servings: 3)

Ingredients

1 cup red lentils, soaked

1 cup squash, peeled, chunks

2 cups vegetable broth

1 teaspoon garlic paste

1 teaspoons salt

¼ cup fried onion

1 teaspoon cayenne pepper

2 tablespoons olive oil

2 tomatoes, chopped

1 teaspoon cumin seeds

1 teaspoon ginger paste

1 tablespoon coriander, chopped

Directions

Fill the Crock-Pot with the lentil, squash, onion, tomatoes, pepper, cumin seeds, ginger garlic paste, vegetable broth, oil, and salt, cove up with a lid.

Let it cook on high for 2 hours.

Put to a serving dish and top with coriander or parsley.

Serve and enjoy.

58. Baked Layered Pizza in Crockpot

(Time: 180 minutes \ Servings: 4)

Ingredients

1 cup ground beef

1 cup tomato ketchup

2 garlic cloves, minced

½ cup tomato sauce

2 large size pita breads

1 teaspoons salt

Few black olives

4 oz. mozzarella cheese, grated

2 tablespoons olive oil

½ cup sour cream, whipped

Directions

Combine the tomato ketchup and the tomato sauce, mix well.

Heat oil in a pan and add mince with garlic, fry until gold color, season with salt, place aside.

Spread one pita bread into a greased Crockpot, top with 4-5 tablespoons of ketchup mixture and place half of the fried mince.

Sprinkle some mozzarella cheese and place another bread, spread tomato ketchup mixture, the remaining mince and sprinkle cheese.

Drizzle some oil and cover the pot with a lid, let it cook on high for 3 hours.

Now remove from the pot and top with olive, some tomatoes and cream. Enjoy.

59. Cabbage with Ground Beef

(Time: 180 minutes \ Servings: 3)

Ingredients

1 can tomatoes

1 cup cabbage, chopped

1 cup ground beef

½ teaspoon garlic paste

2 cups vegetable broth

1 teaspoons salt

1 teaspoon cayenne pepper

2 tablespoons olive oil

½ teaspoon cumin powder

Directions

Fill the Crock-Pot with beef, cabbage, vegetable broth, salt, pepper, oil, cumin powder, , tomatoes and cove up with lid. Let it cook on high for 3 hours on high. Enjoy.

60. Lemon Fish

(Time: 120 minutes \ Servings: 2)

Ingredients

1-2 fish fillets

½ teaspoon black pepper

½ teaspoon garlic powder

½ teaspoon onion powder

3 tablespoons lemon juice

1 teaspoons salt

2 tablespoons olive oil

Directions

In a bowl add the lemon juice, oil, salt, pepper, garlic powder, onion powder and toss to combine. Drizzle over the fish and rub all over it.

Place the fish the into crock-pot and cover with a lid. Let it cook on high for 2 hours on high.

Put to a serving dish and serve and enjoy.

61. Crock Pot Red Bean Gravy

(Time: 420 minutes \ Servings: 8)

Ingredients

1 ½ cup red beans, soaked overnight

½ teaspoon chili powder

¼ teaspoon garlic paste

1 onion chopped

1 cup tomato sauce

2 carrots, peeled, sliced

3 tablespoons lemon juice

1 teaspoons salt

2 tablespoons olive oil

2 inch ginger slice, julienned

4 cups water

Directions

Transfer the water, beans, garlic paste, onion, salt, and chili powder into crock pot, cover with lid and let it cook for 6 hours.

Now open the lid and add in the tomato sauce, carrots and stir, cover again and let it prepare for 1 hour.

Transfer to a serving dish, drizzle lemon juice, and top with julienned ginger. Enjoy.

62. Crock Pot Kale with Green Lentil

(Time: 240 minutes \ Servings: 5)

Ingredients

1 ½ cup lentil, soaked

½ teaspoon black pepper

¼ teaspoon turmeric powder

¼ teaspoon dried coriander powder

1 cup kale leaves, chopped

¼ teaspoon garlic paste

1 onion chopped

2 tomatoes, chopped

1 teaspoons salt

2 tablespoons olive oil

3 cups water

Directions

Transfer the water, lentil, garlic paste, onion, salt, and pepper into crock pot, cover and let it cook for 3 hours.

Add in the tomatoes, kale leaves, and stir, cover again and let it prepare for 1 hour.

Transfer to a serving dish and serve.

63. Red Beans and Corn Salsa

(Time: 420 minutes \ Servings: 4)

Ingredients

1 cup red beans, soaked overnight

1 cup cork kernels, soaked

2 tomatoes, chopped

¼ teaspoon black pepper

3 tablespoons lemon juice

¼ teaspoons salt

1 tablespoon coriander leaves, chopped

4 cups water

Directions

Transfer the water, beans and corn into the Crock Pot, cover with a lid and let it cook for 7 hours. Then remove from the crock-pot and drain out the water.

Transfer the beans and the corn into a bowl and let it cool.

Now combine with the tomatoes, drizzle lemon juice, salt, and pepper. Sprinkle coriander leaves and serve

64. Crock Pot Caramelized Onion

(Time: 120 minutes \ Servings: 3)

Ingredients

4 onion, thinly sliced

½ cup sugar

¼ cup water

1 teaspoon lemon juice

Directions

Turn on the Crock-Pot and add in the water, sugar, lemon juice and stir well until the sugar is dissolved.

Stir continuously until the color of the sugar becomes lightly golden.

Now add the onions and toss.

Cover the crock-pot and let it cook for 2 hours.

Serve and enjoy.

65. Crock Pot Hot Pizza Casserole

(Time: 120 minutes \ Servings: 4)

Ingredients

1 chicken mince

2 garlic cloves, minced

1 cup mozzarella cheese, grated

1 cup tomato sauce

½ cup chili garlic sauce

½ cup parmesan cheese

1 package macaroni, boiled

1 teaspoon oil

Directions

In a skillet heat oil and fry garlic for 20 seconds.

Now add the chicken mince and fry until nicely golden. Place aside.

In the Crock Pot spread macaroni, pour the chili garlic sauce, tomato sauce.

Add the chicken mince and top with grated parmesan and mozzarella cheese.

Transfer to a serving dish and serve.

Enjoy.

66. Crock Pot Peperoni Pizza

(Time: 120 minutes \ Servings: 3)

Ingredients

4 potatoes, peeled, thinly sliced in round shape

1 cup mozzarella cheese, grated

1 cup tomato sauce

1.4 cup peperoni slices

2 onion, thinly sliced

3 teaspoons oil

Directions

In the Crock Pot add oil, potatoes, tomato sauce, pepperoni slices, onion and sprinkle grated cheese. Transfer to a serving dish and enjoy.

67. Crock Pot Spaghetti Pizza

(Time: 120 minutes \ Servings: 3)

Ingredients

1 ground beef

3 garlic cloves, minced

1 package spaghetti, boiled

½ cup ricotta cheese

1 cup mozzarella cheese, grated

½ cup tomato sauce

3 teaspoons oil

Directions

Heat oil in pan and fry garlic for 20 seconds.

Now add the beef and fry until nicely golden. Place aside.

In the Crock pot, add the spaghetti, fried mince, ricotta cheese, tomato sauce and mozzarella cheese.

Transfer to a serving dish and serve.

Enjoy.

68. Crock Pot Black Lentils Velvet Bowl

(Time: 240 minutes \ Servings: 4)

Ingredients

1 cup black lentils

½ cup tomato sauce

1 onion, chopped

1 inch ginger slice, chopped

3 garlic cloves, minced

½ cup sour cream, whipped

¼ cup spring onions, chopped

3 cups water

¼ teaspoon salt

¼ teaspoon black pepper

½ teaspoon cinnamon powder

½ teaspoon cumin powder

2 tablespoons oil

Directions

In the Crock-Pot add the lentils, salt, oil, pepper, water, ginger, cumin powder, cinnamon powder, garlic, onion, tomato sauce and stir.

Let it cook for 4 hours. Now let it cool and transfer to a blender, blend till puree.

Put to a serving bowl and top with sour cream and spring onion. Transfer to a serving dish and serve.

69. Crock Pot Black Beans Salsa

(Time: 360 minutes \ Servings: 4)

Ingredients

1 cup black beans, soaked

2 tomatoes, chopped

1 avocado, peeled, pitted, sliced

¼ teaspoon salt

4 cups water

2 eggs, whisked

2 teaspoon oil

Directions

In the Crock pot add the water and beans, cover with a lid and let it cook for 6 hours.

Now heat oil in pan and add the eggs, fry for 1 minute then flip, keep cooking for 1 minute.

Transfer to a platter and place aside. Now drain off the boiled beans and let it cool.

Combine the beans with tomatoes, avocado and the egg omelette. Enjoy.

70. Chickpea and Beans Stew

(Time: 420 minutes \ Servings: 6)

Ingredients

1 cup black beans, soaked

1 cup chickpea, soaked

2 tomatoes, chopped

1 onion, chopped

2 carrots, sliced

1 inch ginger slice, chopped

3 garlic cloves, minced

4 cups water

¼ teaspoon salt

¼ teaspoon black pepper

½ teaspoon cinnamon powder

½ teaspoon cumin powder

2 tablespoons oil

Directions

Transfer all ingredients into your crock-pot and stir to combine. Cover and let it prepare for 7 hours on high. Ladle to a serving dish and enjoy.

71. Crock Pot Pumpkin Chili Beans

(Time: 420 minutes \ Servings: 6)

Ingredients

1 cup black beans, soaked

2 tomatoes, chopped

1 red bell pepper, chopped

1 cup pumpkin, chunks

1 onion, chopped

½ teaspoon ginger paste

½ teaspoon garlic paste

½ cup sour cream, whipped

4 cups water

¼ teaspoon salt

¼ teaspoon black pepper

½ teaspoon cinnamon powder

3 tablespoons oil

1 teaspoon coriander leaves, chopped

Directions

In the Crock-pot add the beans, salt, oil, pepper, water, ginger, cumin powder, cinnamon powder, garlic, onion, and tomatoes, stir.

Place and cook for 6 hours on high temperature.

Now add in the pumpkin chunks and the bell pepper, stir well and let it cook again for 1 hour. Transfer to a serving dish and top with sour cream. Sprinkle coriander leaves.

72. Tropical Quinoa Corn Chili

(Time: 180 minutes \ Servings: 4)

Ingredients

1 cup quinoa

2 tomatoes, chopped

2 red bell peppers, chopped

1 cup corn kernels

½ teaspoon garlic paste

4 cups water

¼ teaspoon salt

¼ teaspoon black pepper

3 tablespoons oil

Directions

Fill your crock-pot with all the ingredients and mix well. Cover with a lid and let it cook for 3 hours. Put to a serving dish and enjoy.

73. Crock Pot Corn

(Time: 300 minutes \ Servings: 4)

Ingredients

3-4 corns

5 cups water

1 teaspoon salt

1 tablespoon lemon juice

¼ teaspoon black pepper

Directions

In the Crock-pot add water, salt and corns, stir and cover up with a lid.

Now let it cook for 5 hours.

Transfer to a serving platter and drizzle lemon juice.

Sprinkle black pepper and serve.

Enjoy.

74. Beans and Avocado Salsa

(Time: 420 minutes \ Servings: 4)

Ingredients

1 cup red beans, soaked

1 cup corn kernels

2 tomatoes, chopped

2 carrots, chopped

2 teaspoon coriander leaves, chopped

1 onion sliced

2 avocados, peeled, pitted, sliced

2 tablespoons apple cider vinegar

2 tablespoons honey

½ teaspoon caster sugar

1 pinch salt

¼ teaspoon lemon juice

4 cups water

Directions

In the Crock-pot add beans, water, and stir. Let it cook for 7 hours.

Drain off the water and let the beans and corn cool.

Combine the beans and corn with the tomatoes, carrots, coriander leaves, honey, onion, sugar, salt, lemon juice, vinegar, and avocado, toss everything. Place into a serving dish.

75. Chickpea and Tomato Salsa

(Time: 420 minutes \ Servings: 6)

Ingredients

1 chickpeas, soaked

3 tomatoes, chopped

¼ teaspoon salt

1 teaspoon coriander leaves, chopped

¼ teaspoon thyme, chopped

2 tablespoon lemon juice

¼ teaspoon black pepper

3 cups water

Directions

In the Crock-pot add the chickpea and water, let it cook for 7 hours. Drain off the water and let the chickpea cool well.

In a bowl, add the chickpeas, tomatoes, salt, lemon juice, coriander leaves, thyme, and pepper, toss to combine. Enjoy.

Crock-Pot Chicken Recipes

76. Crock-Pot Chicken Roast

(Time: 420 minutes \ Servings: 6)

Ingredients

1 whole chicken
1 teaspoon garlic paste
½ teaspoon ginger powder
1 teaspoon salt
½ teaspoon cinnamon powder
1 teaspoon cayenne pepper

2 tablespoon lemon juice
2 tablespoon vinegar
¼ teaspoon black pepper
¼ teaspoon cinnamon powder
2 tablespoons olive oil

Directions

In a bowl add all ingredients and mix well. Pour over the chicken and rub all over the chicken and place inside the crock-pot.

Cover the pot with a lid and let it cook for 7 hours on high. Serve hot and enjoy.

77. Chicken White Korma

(Time: 120 minutes \ Servings: 4)

Ingredients

4 oz. chicken boneless, pieces
1 cup sour cream
½ cup ricotta cheese
1 teaspoon garlic paste
1 teaspoon salt

¼ teaspoon black pepper
1 package pasta, boiled
1 teaspoon coriander, chopped
2 tablespoons olive oil

Directions

Transfer the chicken with the cheese, sour cream, garlic, pepper and salt, mix well.

Place the cover on the pot and let it cook on high for 2 hours.

Place the pasta into a serving platter and top with chicken korma. Sprinkle coriander as much you like. Serve hot and enjoy.

78. Crock-Pot Chicken Lasanga

(Time: 120 minutes \ Servings: 8)

Ingredients

1 cup chicken mince

5-6 lasagna strips, boiled

1 teaspoon garlic paste

2 cups tomato sauce

½ cup tomato ketchup

2 tablespoons olive oil

Directions

Heat oil in a pan and fry garlic for 20 seconds. Now add the chicken and fry till lightly golden. Season with salt and pour in the tomato sauce and tomato ketchup, let it simmer for 5 minutes.

Arrange 1-2 lasagna strips on the bottom of your Crockpot and spread 3-4 tablespoons of fried mince mixture. Now place 1-2 more lasagna strips and spread 2-3 tablespoons of mince mixture. Repeat the same steps for all strips.

Cover the pot with a lid and leave it cook for 2 hours. Serve and enjoy.

79. Lemon Chicken Breasts

(Time: 180 minutes \ Servings: 4)

Ingredients

4 chicken breasts

2 tablespoon soya sauce

1 teaspoon garlic paste

1 teaspoon salt

1 teaspoon black pepper

2 tablespoon lemon juice

½ teaspoon lemon zest

2 tablespoons vinegar

2 tablespoons olive oil

1 package noodles, boiled

Directions

In a bowl add oil, lemon juice, salt, pepper, lemon zest, vinegar, garlic, and soya sauce, mix well. Add in the chicken breasts and toss until well combined.

Transfer the chicken into a greased crock-pot and leave it cook for 3 hours.

Serve with boiled noodles.

80. Chicken Mac Stew

(Time: 180 minutes \ Servings: 4)

Ingredients

4 oz. chicken, boneless

1 package macaroni

1 teaspoon garlic powder

1 teaspoon thyme

1 can tomatoes

1 teaspoon salt

1 teaspoon black pepper

2 tablespoon lemon juice

2 tablespoons olive oil

4 cups chicken broth

Directions

In the Crock Pot add all the ingredients and mix well. Cover the crock-pot and leave it cook for 3 hours. Serve hot.

81. Pulled Chicken Burger

(Time: 180 minutes \ Servings: 3)

Ingredients

3 oz. chicken, boneless, pieces

2 tablespoon soya sauce

1 cup chili garlic sauce

2-3 garlic cloves, minced

1 teaspoon salt

1 teaspoon cayenne pepper

2 tablespoon lemon juice

2 tablespoon red wine vinegar

2 tablespoons olive oil

3-4 buns, halved

2 cup hot water

Directions

In the crock-pot add the chicken, water, oil, pepper, salt and garlic, let it cook for 3 hours on high. Now shred the chicken with a fork and place aside.

Combine the chili garlic sauce with the shredded chicken, soya sauce, lemon juice, and vinegar. Microwave buns for 2-3 seconds.

Place 4-5 tbsp of the chicken mixture into centre of 2 bun slices. Do the same for all buns.

82. Ground Chicken Chili with Red Beans

(Time: 420 minutes \ Servings: 6)

Ingredients

2 cups chicken mince

2 cups red beans, soaked

2 tablespoon soya sauce

2 cups tomato sauce

2 tablespoon barbecue sauce

1 red bell pepper, chopped

1 teaspoon garlic paste

1 teaspoon salt

1 teaspoon chili powder

2 tablespoon lemon juice

2 tablespoons olive oil

Directions

Heat oil in a pan and fry garlic with the chicken for about 5-10 minutes.

Now put to a bowl and place aside.

In the crock-pot add the beans, salt, chili powder, and mix well. Cook for 6 hours.

Now add in the fried chicken, bell pepper, tomato sauce, barbecue sauce, and soya sauce, and cook again for 1 hour. Transfer to a serving bowl and drizzle lemon juice and enjoy.

83. Coconut Chicken Tendered

(Time: 120 minutes \ Servings: 6)

Ingredients

3 chicken breasts

1 cup coconut milk

2 tablespoons honey

1 cup sour cream

¼ teaspoon black pepper

1 teaspoon salt

2 tablespoons olive oil

Directions

In the crock pot add all ingredients and mix them well. Let it cook on high temperature for 2 hours. Place to a serving platter and serve with boiled rice and sprinkle with parsley.

84. Crock Pot Tandoori Chicken

(Time: 120 minutes \ Servings: 4)

Ingredients

4 oz. chicken, boneless, pieces

1 cup yogurt

¼ teaspoon turmeric powder

1 teaspoon barbecue spice

2 tablespoons tomato sauce

1 teaspoon garlic powder

¼ teaspoon salt

¼ teaspoon chili powder

2 tablespoon lemon juice

2 tablespoons olive oil

Directions

In the crock-pot add the chicken, yogurt, garlic, barbecue spice, turmeric powder, tomato sauce, salt, chili powder, and mix well. Leave it cook for 2 hours.

Serve with boiled rice and top with lemon juice.

85. Chicken Vegie Stew

(Time: 180 minutes \ Servings: 4)

Ingredients

4 oz. chicken, boneless, pieces

1 cup green beans, trimmed

2 tablespoon soya sauce

2 carrots, sliced

2-3 garlic cloves, minced

¼ teaspoon turmeric powder

¼ teaspoon salt

¼ teaspoon chili powder

¼ teaspoon turmeric powder

2 tablespoon lemon juice

2 tablespoons olive oil

2 cups chicken broth

Directions

In the Crock-pot add al ingredients and toss to combine. Cook for 3 hours. Serve with boiled rice or bread and Enjoy.

86. Chicken Mushroom Jingle

(Time: 180 minutes \ Servings: 4)

Ingredients

2 chicken breasts

¼ cup soya sauce

1 cup mushrooms, sliced

1 tablespoon garlic powder

¼ teaspoon salt

¼ teaspoon chili powder

2 tablespoon lemon juice

2 tablespoons olive oil

Directions

In the Crock-pot add all ingredients and mix thoroughly. Cook for 3 hours.

Put to a serving dish and serve hot.

87. Mustard Chicken Mushroom

(Time: 120 minutes \ Servings: 4)

Ingredients

2 chicken breasts

2 teaspoon Dijon mustard

1 cup mushrooms, sliced

1 tablespoon garlic paste

¼ teaspoon salt

½ cup fried onion

¼ teaspoon black pepper

¼ teaspoon cinnamon powder

1 pinch turmeric powder

¼ teaspoon cumin powder

2 tablespoons olive oil

Directions

In the Crock-pot add the chicken, mustard, garlic, onion, mushrooms, turmeric, cinnamon powder, cumin powder, pepper, salt, and mix thoroughly.

Let to cook for 2 hours.

Transfer to a serving dish and serve hot.

Enjoy.

88. Creamy Chicken Gravy

(Time: 120 minutes \ Servings: 4)

Ingredients

2 chicken breasts

¼ cup mayonnaise

1 cup sour cream

1 tablespoon garlic powder

¼ cup green onion, chopped

¼ teaspoon salt

½ cup chicken soup

¼ teaspoon chili powder

2 tablespoons olive oil

Directions

In the crock-pot add the chicken, cream, salt, chicken soup, and pepper, let it cook for 30 minutes on high. Now add in mayonnaise, garlic powder, mix well.

Transfer to a serving dish and sprinkle green onion. Enjoy it.

89. Chicken Ginger Roast

(Time: 180 minutes \ Servings: 4)

Ingredients

2-3 chicken breasts

1 teaspoon ginger paste

¼ teaspoon garlic paste

1 teaspoon thyme

1 teaspoon cinnamon powder

½ teaspoon cumin powder

¼ teaspoon onion powder

¼ teaspoon salt

¼ teaspoon chili powder

2 tablespoons olive oil

Directions

In a bowl add all ingredients and mix well.

Pour over the chicken and rub gently with hands on the chicken.

Place the chicken breasts inside the crock-pot and let it cook for 3 hours on high temperature.

Transfer to a serving dish and enjoy.

90. Ground Chicken Macaroni

(Time: 180 minutes \ Servings: 4)

Ingredients

1 cup chicken mince

1 package macaroni

1 cup tomato sauce

2 tablespoons soya sauce

1 onion, chopped

1 tablespoon garlic powder

¼ teaspoon salt

½ cup chicken soup

¼ teaspoon chili powder

2 tablespoons olive oil

2 cups chicken broth

Directions

Heat oil in a pan and fry chicken for 5-6 minutes on high temperature. Place aside.

Now transfer the macaroni, chicken, tomato sauce, soya sauce, salt, chili powder, garlic powder, and chicken broth into crock-pot, mix well.

Let it cook on high for 3 hours. Enjoy.

91. Baked Chicken Loaf

(Time: 180 minutes \ Servings: 4)

Ingredients

2 chicken breasts

1 cup bread crumbs

1 teaspoon thyme

1 teaspoon black pepper

1 tablespoon garlic powder

¼ teaspoon salt

2 eggs, whisked

2 tablespoons olive oil

Directions

In a bowl add the bread crumbs, salt, pepper, garlic powder, thyme and mix well.

Dip each chicken breast into the eggs then roll out into bread crumbs.

Transfer to greased crock-pot and cover up with lid. Let it cook for 3 hours on high.

Transfer to a serving dish and serve with desired sauce.

92. Crock-Pot Chicken Casserole

(Time: 180 minutes \ Servings: 6)

Ingredients

1 cup chicken, boiled, shredded

1 teaspoon garlic powder

2 cups tomato sauce

2 oz. mozzarella cheese, shredded

1 cup parmesan cheese, shredded

Directions

In the Crock-Pot add the chicken and pour the tomato sauce, spread all over in the pot.

Top with mozzarella cheese, parmesan cheese and sprinkle garlic powder.

Cover the pot and let it cook for 3 hours on high. Serve and enjoy.

93 Crock-Pot Chicken and Potato Afritada

(Time: 300 minutes \ Servings: 4)

Ingredients

4 oz. chicken, boneless

4 large potatoes, peeled, diced

1 teaspoon black pepper

¼ teaspoon salt

1 teaspoon garlic paste

2 cups tomato sauce

Few coriander leaves, chopped

2 tablespoons olive oil

Directions

Put all ingredients into the Crock-Pot and place a lid.

Set the pot on high for 5 hours.

Transfer to a serving dish and top with coriander.

Serve and enjoy.

94. Crock-Pot Chicken Yogurt Masala

(Time: 240 minutes \ Servings: 5)

Ingredients

5 oz. chicken, boneless, pieces

2 cups yogurt

¼ teaspoon turmeric powder

1 teaspoon black pepper

¼ teaspoon salt

1 teaspoon ginger paste

2 tablespoons olive oil

Directions

Transfer all ingredients in the Crock-Pot and place a lid.

Set the Crock-pot on high for 4 hours. Put to a serving dish and serve with boiled rice.

95. Crock-Pot Peanut Chicken

(Time: 180 minutes \ Servings: 3)

Ingredients

4 oz. chicken, boneless, pieces

1 cup peanuts

2 tablespoon soya sauce

1 teaspoon black pepper

¼ teaspoon salt

1 teaspoon ginger paste

¼ teaspoon garlic powder

2 tablespoons olive oil

Directions

Transfer all ingredients into the Crock-Pot and place a lid.

Set the Crock-pot on high for 3 hours.

Put to serving dish and serve with rice.

96. Crock-Pot Chicken Chickpea Chowder

(Time: 420 minutes \ Servings: 3)

Ingredients

4 oz. chicken, boneless, pieces

1 cup chickpea, soaked

¼ teaspoon turmeric powder

½ cup tomato sauce

2 tablespoon soya sauce

1 teaspoon black pepper

¼ teaspoon salt

1 teaspoon ginger paste

¼ teaspoon garlic powder

2 tablespoons olive oil

4 cups water

Directions

Transfer the chickpea, water, salt, ginger garlic paste and pepper into crockpot, stir and let it cook for 6 hours on high.

Now add the chicken, oil, tomato sauce, turmeric powder, and mix.

Let it cook for 1 hour. Serve with rice and enjoy.

97. Chicken Spinach Orzo

(Time: 180 minutes \ Servings: 3)

Ingredients

4 oz. chicken, boneless, pieces

1 cup orzo

¼ cup spinach, chopped

½ cup sour cream

1 teaspoon black pepper

¼ teaspoon cumin seeds

¼ teaspoon salt

2-3 garlic cloves, minced

2 tablespoons olive oil

2 cups water

Directions

Transfer all ingredients into the crock-pot and place a lid.

Set the Crock-pot on high for 3 hours. Remove from the pot and put to a serving dish.

Serve and enjoy.

98. Chicken Chili Orzo Casserole

(Time: 240 minutes \ Servings: 6)

Ingredients

5 oz. chicken, boneless, small pieces

2 cups orzo

¼ cup spinach, chopped

1 potato, peeled, sliced

3 bell peppers, chopped

½ cup fried onion

¼ teaspoon chili powder

¼ teaspoon cumin powder

¼ teaspoon salt

2-3 garlic cloves, minced

2 tablespoons olive oil

4 cups chicken broth

Directions

Transfer all ingredients into the crock-pot and place a lid.

Set the Crock-pot on high for 4 hours.

Transfer to a serving dish and serve hot.

99. Chicken Peas Pasta

(Time: 180 minutes \ Servings: 3)

Ingredients

4 oz. chicken, boneless, pieces

1 cup peas

1 package pasta

½ cup sour cream

2 tablespoons tomato ketchup

3 cups chicken broth

1 teaspoon black pepper

¼ teaspoon salt

2-3 garlic cloves, minced

2 tablespoons olive oil

Directions

Transfer the chicken, chicken broth, salt and pepper into crock pot, let it cook for 1 hour on a high temperature.

Now shred the chicken and add in the peas, ketchup, cream, pasta, garlic, oil and let it cook again for 2 hours. Put to a serving dish and serve.

100. Steamed Chicken Spinach

(Time: 240 minutes \ Servings: 4)

Ingredients

4 oz. chicken, boneless, pieces

1 cup spinach leaves

¼ cup cherry tomatoes, halved

½ cup soya sauce

1 teaspoon black pepper

¼ teaspoon salt

2 tablespoons lemon juice

1 teaspoon garlic powder

2 tablespoons olive oil

2 cups water

Directions

Transfer the chicken, spinach, tomatoes, soya sauce, pepper, salt, garlic powder, lemon juice, and oil in baking dish, toss well.

Add water into the crock-pot and place a baking dish into the pot, cover up with a lid and let it cook for 4 hours on high.

Serve hot and enjoy.

Crock-Pot Meat Recipes

101. Crock-Pot Lamb Vindaloo

(Time: 420 minutes \ Servings: 8)

Ingredients

8 oz. lamb meat

1 teaspoon garlic paste

1 teaspoon ginger paste

2 red chilies

¼ cup vinegar

2 tablespoon lemon juice

2 tablespoons oil

¼ cup yogurt

1 teaspoon salt

2 cups vegetable broth

½ teaspoon cinnamon powder

1 teaspoon cayenne pepper

¼ teaspoon cinnamon powder

Directions

In a blender add the vinegar, red chilies, yogurt, salt, oil, lemon juice, ginger garlic paste, cumin powder, vegetable broth, and cinnamon powder, blend until it becomes puree.

Transfer the lamb meat into the crock-pot and drizzle blended sauce.

Cover the pot with a lid and let it cook for 7 hours on high.

Transfer to a serving dish and serve with rice.

Enjoy.

102. Hot and Spicy Beef Masala

(Time: 420 minutes \ Servings: 6)

Ingredients

8 oz. beef, pieces

1 teaspoon garlic paste

1 teaspoon ginger paste

¼ teaspoon chili powder

4 tablespoon soya sauce

¼ cup tomato sauce

2 tablespoons vinegar

3 tablespoons oil

1 teaspoon salt

½ cup Worcestershire sauce

3 cups vegetable broth

Directions

Put all ingredients into the Crock-Pot and place a lid. Set the Crock-pot on high for 7 hours. Transfer to a serving dish and serve with rice. Enjoy.

103. Crock-Pot Beef Steak

(Time: 420 minutes \ Servings: 6)

Ingredients

6-8 oz. beef steaks

1 teaspoon garlic paste

4 tablespoon soya sauce

3 tablespoons oil

1 teaspoon salt

½ cup Worcestershire sauce

Directions

Place the beef steak into the crock-pot and pour the Worcestershire sauce, soya sauce, oil; mix well.

Put the garlic into the pot and combine well.

Set the pot on high for 7 hours.

Serve and enjoy.

104. Beef Potato Adobo

(Time: 420 minutes \ Servings: 6)

Ingredients

8 oz. beef, pieces

1 green bell pepper, sliced

2-3 garlic cloves minced

2 potatoes, peeled, diced

2 carrots, peeled, sliced

2 tablespoons vinegar

3 tablespoons oil

¼ cup yogurt

1 teaspoon salt

3 cups vegetable broth

Directions

Put all ingredients into the crock-pot, place the lid and set the Crock-pot on high for 7 hours.

Transfer to a serving dish and serve hot.

105. Crock Pot Sizzling Lamb Leg

(Time: 480 minutes \ Servings: 4)

Ingredients

1 lamb leg

2 tablespoons garlic paste

1 teaspoon ginger paste

2 tablespoons vinegar

½ cup soya sauce

½ cup barbecue sauce

4 tablespoon Worcestershire sauce

2 tablespoons oil

1 teaspoon salt

Directions

In a bowl add all ingredients and mix well.

Put the lamb leg into the crock-pot and pour sauce over it, combine everything.

Place a lid on the crock-pot and set it on low for 8 hours.

Transfer to a serving dish and serve hot.

Enjoy.

106. Lamb Shanks

(Time: 420 minutes \ Servings: 6)

Ingredients

6 oz. lamb shanks

¼ cup tomato sauce

2-3 garlic cloves minced

2 tablespoons balsamic vinegar

3 tablespoons oil

1 teaspoon salt

2 cups vegetable broth

Directions

Put all ingredients into the Crock-pot, place a lid and set it on high for 7 hours.

Transfer to a serving dish and serve hot.

107. Beef Kebabs

(Time: 420 minutes \ Servings: 6)

Ingredients

2 cups ground beef

2 tablespoon coriander, chopped

2 bread slices, roughly shredded

1 teaspoon garlic paste

3 tablespoons oil

1 teaspoon salt

1 teaspoon chili powder

1 onion, chopped

Directions

In a bowl add the ground beef, coriander, bread, salt, chili powder, garlic paste, and onion, mix well.

Take 4-5 tablespoons of the mixture into your hand and crape around a toothpick to form a kebab shape. Make all kebabs following the same steps.

Place into a greased crock-pot, place a lid and set the Crock-pot on high for 7 hours.

Transfer to a serving dish and serve hot.

Enjoy.

108. Beef and Potato Gravy

(Time: 420 minutes \ Servings: 6)

Ingredients

8 oz. beef, pieces

2 cups tomato sauce

2-3 garlic cloves minced

2 potatoes, peeled, diced

2 carrots, peeled, sliced

2 tablespoons vinegar

3 tablespoons oil

1 teaspoon salt

3 cups vegetable broth

½ teaspoon chili powder

Directions

Put all ingredients into the Crock-pot, place a lid and set it on high for 7 hours.

Transfer to a serving dish and serve hot.

109. Beef Tika

(Time: 420 minutes \ Servings: 6)

Ingredients

6 oz. beef, pieces

½ cup yogurt

1 teaspoon garlic paste

2 tablespoons vinegar

3 tablespoons oil

1 tablespoon soya sauce

1 teaspoon black pepper

1 teaspoon salt

Directions

In a bowl add the beef, salt, garlic, yogurt, vinegar, oil, and pepper.

Let it marinade for about 30-40 minutes.

Now transfer the beef with the marinade into the crock-pot, cover with a lid and set it on high for 7 hours.

Transfer to a serving dish and serve hot.

110. Beef Loafs

(Time: 420 minutes \ Servings: 6)

Ingredients

6-8 oz. beef steak

1 teaspoon garlic paste

1 teaspoon ginger powder

4 tablespoons soya sauce

2 tablespoons oyster sauce

3 tablespoons oil

1 teaspoon salt

2 tablespoons Worcestershire sauce

1 tablespoon vinegar

Directions

In a bowl add the beef, oyster sauce, vinegar, Worcestershire sauce, soya sauce, oil and mix well. Wrap the beef into an aluminum foil and place inside the crock pot.

Set it on high for 7 hour. Now cut the beef with sharp knife. Serve and enjoy.

111. Crock Pot Beef Barbecue

(Time: 420 minutes \ Servings: 6)

Ingredients

6-8 oz. beef, boneless, pieces

1 teaspoon garlic paste

1 teaspoon ginger paste

2 tablespoons soya sauce

½ cup barbecue sauce

2 tablespoons oil

1 teaspoon salt

2 tablespoons red wine vinegar

2 tablespoon dill, chopped

2 tablespoons Worcestershire sauce

Directions

Put all ingredients into the Crock-pot and combine well.

Adjust the crock-pot on high for 7 hour.

Serve and enjoy.

112. Beef and Tomato Gravy

(Time: 420 minutes \ Servings: 6)

Ingredients

4-5 oz. beef, pieces

4 tomatoes, chopped

¼ cup fried onion

1 teaspoon garlic paste

3 tablespoons oil

½ teaspoon chili powder

1 teaspoon salt

1 tablespoon vinegar

½ teaspoon cumin powder

½ teaspoon cinnamon powder

¼ teaspoon turmeric powder

2 cups water

Directions

In the Crock Pot add the water, garlic paste, oil, salt, and beef, mix and let it cook on high for 6 hours.

Now add the tomatoes, turmeric powder, chili powder, vinegar, and onion, cook again for another hour. Transfer to a serving dish and sprinkle cinnamon and cumin powder.

113. Ground Beef Red Hot Curry

(Time: 420 minutes \ Servings: 6)

Ingredients

1 cup ground beef

1 teaspoon garlic paste

½ cup ginger juice

2 cup tomato sauce

1 can tomatoes

1 cup white beans

3 tablespoons oil

1 teaspoon salt

¼ teaspoon chili powder

1 tablespoon coriander leaves, chopped

4 cups water

Directions

In the Crock pot add the beans, salt, and water, let it cook for 6 hours on low.

Heat oil in a pan and fry the ground beef with garlic for 4-5 minutes.

Transfer the ground beef to the Crock pot with the tomato sauce, ginger juice, can tomatoes, chili powder, and stir. Set to high for an hour.

Put to a serving dish and top with chopped coriander. Serve and enjoy.

114. Beef Mince and Beans

(Time: 420 minutes \ Servings: 6)

Ingredients

2 cups beef mince

2 cups red beans, soaked

2 cups tomato sauce

1 teaspoon garlic paste

1 teaspoon salt

1 teaspoon chili powder

2 tablespoon lemon juice

2 tablespoons olive oil

1 oz. cheese, grated

Directions

Heat oil in a pan and fry garlic with beef mince for about 5-10 minutes.

Put to a bowl and place aside. In the Crock-pot add the beans, salt, chili powder, and stir well. Cover and let it cook for 6 hours on high.

Now add the fried beef and tomato sauce, cook again for 1 hour. Put to a serving dish and top with cheese slices, drizzle lemon juice. Serve and enjoy.

115. Beef Chowder with Green Beans

(Time: 420 minutes \ Servings: 6)

Ingredients

4 oz. beef, pieces

1 bunch green beans, trimmed

3 tomatoes, chopped

1 teaspoon garlic paste

¼ cup fried onion

1 teaspoon salt

1 teaspoon chili powder

¼ teaspoon turmeric powder

2 tablespoon lemon juice

2 tablespoons olive oil

3 cups water

1 bay leaf

Directions

In the crock-pot add the water, salt, fried onion, bay leaf, turmeric powder, chili powder, beef, and garlic, mix well. Cover and cook for 6 hours on high.

Now add the tomatoes, beans, let it cook again for another hour. Place in a serving dish and drizzle lemon juice. Serve and enjoy.

116. Carrot and Potato Beef Adobo

(Time: 420 minutes \ Servings: 6)

Ingredients

8 oz. beef, pieces, boneless

1 teaspoon garlic paste

1 cup tomato puree

½ cup baby potatoes, halved

2 carrots, peeled, cut into 2 inch slices

3 tablespoons oil

1 teaspoon salt

3 cups chicken broth

½ teaspoon black pepper

½ teaspoon cinnamon powder

¼ teaspoon cumin powder

Directions

Transfer all ingredients into the Crock-pot, cover up with a lid and set it on high for 7 hours. Put to a serving dish and serve hot. Enjoy.

117. Beef and Chickpea Curry Masala

(Time: 420 minutes \ Servings: 8)

Ingredients

4 oz. beef, small pieces, boneless

1 teaspoon garlic paste

2 onions, sliced

2 green bell peppers, sliced

2 cups chickpea, soaked

2 tomatoes, chopped

3 potatoes, cut into small cubes

3 tablespoons oil

1 teaspoon salt

3 cups vegetable broth

½ teaspoon chili powder

½ teaspoon cinnamon powder

¼ teaspoon cumin powder

Directions

Transfer all ingredients into the crock-pot, cover up with a lid and set it on high for 7 hours. Put to a serving dish and serve hot.

118. Ground Beef Loaded Burger

(Time: 120 minutes \ Servings: 3)

Ingredients

1 cup ground beef

1 can tomatoes

2-3 garlic cloves, minced

1 teaspoon salt

1 teaspoon cayenne pepper

2 tablespoon lemon juice

2 tablespoons olive oil

3-4 buns, halved

1 cup water

Directions

In the Crock-pot add the ground beef, salt, water, lemon juice, can tomatoes, oil, pepper, and garlic, cook for 2 hours on high. Stir occasionally after 30 minutes.

When it's done, transfer to a bowl and let it cool a little. Microwave the buns for 2-3 seconds. Place 5-6 tablespoons of beef mixture into centre of 2 bun slices.

Repeat the steps for all buns.

119. Honey and Pepper Beef Steaks

(Time: 420 minutes \ Servings: 8)

Ingredients

6-8 oz. beef steaks

1 teaspoon garlic powder

½ teaspoon ginger powder

2 tablespoon soya sauce

3 tablespoons honey

3 tablespoons oil

1 teaspoon salt

1 teaspoon black pepper

Directions

In a zipping bag add the garlic powder, ginger powder, salt, pepper, oil, honey, soya sauce and shake to mix. Now add in the beef steaks and shake again.

Let it sit for 30 minutes. Place the beef steak into the Crock and set the pot on high for 6-7 hours.

Serve and enjoy.

120. Honey Flavoured Beef Mooch

(Time: 420 minutes \ Servings: 6)

Ingredients

6 oz. beef, small pieces, boneless

1 teaspoon garlic powder

¼ cup honey

3 tablespoons oil

1 teaspoon salt

2 cups vegetable broth

¼ cup Worcestershire sauce

Directions

Put the beef, vegetable broth, salt, garlic powder, and oil into the crock-pot, cover up with lid and set crock-pot on high for 6 hours.

Now add in the Worcestershire sauce and the honey and mix well.

Let it cook for 1 hour on high temperature. Transfer to a serving dish and serve hot.

121. Meat Pasta Curry

(Time: 420 minutes \ Servings: 4)

Ingredients

4 oz. beef, small pieces, boneless

1 package pasta

2-3 garlic cloves, minced

3 tablespoons oil

1 teaspoon salt

3 cups vegetable broth

1 cup tomato sauce

Directions

Put the beef, vegetable broth, pasta, salt, garlic, tomato sauce, and oil into the Crock-pot, cover up with a lid and set it on high for 7 hours.

Transfer to a serving dish and serve hot.

122. Meat Lava Burger

(Time: 420 minutes \ Servings: 4)

Ingredients

4 oz. beef, boneless, cut into 1 inch this strips

2-3 garlic cloves, minced

¼ cup soya sauce

½ cup Worcestershire sauce

1 teaspoon salt

2 tablespoon lemon juice

2 tablespoons olive oil

3-4 buns, halved

1 cup water

Directions

In the Crock-pot add the ground beef, water, oil, and garlic, leave to cook for 6 hours on high.

Now add in the soya sauce, Worcestershire sauce, lemon juice, and mix well.

Cook again for 1 hour.

Now transfer to a bowl and let to cool a little.

Microwave the buns for 2-3 seconds.

Place 5-6 tablespoons of the cooked beef between the 2 bun slices.

Repeat the steps for all buns.

123. Beef Chili Shashlik

(Time: 420 minutes \ Servings: 4)

Ingredients

4 oz. beef, boneless, small pieces

2 bell peppers, sliced

2 tablespoon soya sauce

1 tablespoon coriander, chopped

4-5 garlic cloves, minced

1 teaspoon salt

½ teaspoon black pepper

2 tablespoon lemon juice

2 tablespoons olive oil

1 cups water

1 onion, chopped

¼ cup mushrooms, sliced

Directions

In the Crock-pot add the beef, mushrooms, pepper, soya sauce, coriander, water, oil, and garlic, leave it cook for 6 hours on high.

Now add the bell pepper, lemon juice, and mix well.

Cook again for 1 hour.

Serve with boiled rice.

124. Meat Tandoors with Pasta

(Time: 420 minutes \ Servings: 4)

Ingredients

4 oz. beef, steaks,

1 package pasta, boiled

2-3 garlic cloves, minced

3 tablespoons oil

1 teaspoon salt

2 cups vegetable broth

½ cup soya sauce

¼ teaspoon Dijon Mustard

½ teaspoon black pepper

1 tablespoon lime juice

1 teaspoon onion powder

Directions

Put the beef, vegetable broth, mustard, lime juice, pepper, onion powder, soya sauce, salt, garlic, and oil into the Crock-pot, cover up with a lid and set it on high for 7 hours.

Spread the paste into a serving platter and serve with cooked meat tandoors.

125. Tropical Tomato Sauce Cooked Meatballs

(Time: 420 minutes \ Servings: 12)

Ingredients

2 cups ground beef

2 bread slices, roughly shredded

1 teaspoon garlic paste

3 tablespoons oil

1 teaspoon salt

1 teaspoon chili powder

1 onion, chopped

3 cups tomato sauce

¼ teaspoon chili powder

Directions

In a bowl add the ground beef, bread, salt, chili powder, garlic paste, and onion, mix well.

Make small round balls with mixture and insert toothpick to each meatball.

Pour the tomato sauce and oil into the crock pot and sprinkle chili powder, stir.

Put the meatballs into the pot.

Cover up with a lid and set it on high for 7 hours.

Transfer to a serving dish and serve hot.

Crock-Pot Vegetable Recipes

126. Steamed Zucchini Sprouts

(Time: 240 minutes \ Servings: 6)

Ingredients

3 large zucchini, sliced

4 oz. Brussels sprouts

1 teaspoon garlic powder

½ teaspoon onion powder

1 teaspoon ginger powder

¼ teaspoon chili flakes

2 tablespoon lemon juice

¼ teaspoon black pepper

½ teaspoon salt

Directions

In a baking dish add the zucchini, Brussels sprouts, and sprinkle garlic powder, chili flakes, salt, ginger powder, black pepper, onion powder, and mix well.

Now add 2 cups of water into the Crock pot and place a baking dish inside the pot.

Cover it with a lid and let it cook for 4 hours on high.

Transfer to a serving dish and drizzle lemon juice.

Enjoy.

127. Maple Roasted Lime Sweet Potatoes

(Time: 240 minutes \ Servings: 5)

Ingredients

4 oz. sweet potatoes, peeled, sliced

1 teaspoon ginger powder

¼ cup maple syrup

2 tablespoon lemon juice

¼ teaspoon black pepper

½ teaspoon salt

Directions

Transfer the sweet potatoes, salt, pepper, maple syrup and ginger powder into the Crock pot, combine well. Cover the pot with a lid and let it cook for 4 hours on high.

Transfer to a serving dish and drizzle lemon juice. Enjoy.

128. Cauliflower and Chickpea Curry

(Time: 420 minutes \ Servings: 6)

Ingredients

2 cups cauliflower florets

1 cup chickpea, soaked

1 cup spinach leaves, chopped

1 teaspoon garlic paste

1 onion, chopped

¼ teaspoon turmeric powder

½ cup chicken soup

2 tablespoon lemon juice

½ teaspoon salt

2 cups water

¼ teaspoon black pepper

Directions

In your crock-pot add the chickpea, water, and salt, let it cook for 4 hours on high.

Now add in the cauliflower, garlic, spinach, turmeric powder, black pepper, chicken soup, and mix well.

Cover the pot with a lid and let it cook for 2 hours on high.

Transfer to a serving dish and drizzle lemon juice.

129. Crock-Pot Roasted Bacon Potatoes

(Time: 240 minutes \ Servings: 6)

Ingredients

4 large potatoes, thinly sliced

¼ cup dried bacon

½ teaspoon garlic powder

2 teaspoons oil

2 tablespoon lemon juice

½ teaspoon salt

½ teaspoon black pepper

1 teaspoon coriander, chopped

Directions

In your Crock-pot add the potatoes, pepper, garlic powder, oil, and salt, stir well and let it cook for 4 hours on high. Now transfer to a serving platter and sprinkle bacon and coriander. Drizzle lemon juice on top and serve hot.

130. Thyme Flavored Roasted Potatoes

(Time: 420 minutes \ Servings: 6)

Ingredients

2 oz. potatoes, halved

1 tablespoon thyme

¼ teaspoon black pepper

2 teaspoons oil

2 tablespoon lemon juice

½ teaspoon salt

¼ teaspoon dried coriander powder

¼ teaspoon cumin powder

Directions

In your Crock-pot add the potatoes, thyme, coriander powder, cumin powder, pepper, oil, and salt, stir well and let it cook for 6 hours on high.

Now transfer to a serving dish and drizzle lemon juice on top.

Serve hot and enjoy.

131. Vinegar Pickled Potatoes

(Time: 180 minutes \ Servings: 4)

Ingredients

6-8 potatoes, diced

¼ teaspoon black pepper

¼ cup vinegar

½ teaspoon salt

Directions

In your Crock-pot add the potatoes, vinegar, salt, and pepper, stir well and cook for 3 hours on high. Now transfer to a serving dish and enjoy.

132. Vegetable Chickpea and Beans Salad

(Time: 420 minutes \ Servings: 4)

Ingredients

1 cup chickpea, soaked

1 cup red beans, soaked

¼ teaspoon black pepper

1 teaspoons oil

2 tablespoon lemon juice

2 tablespoons balsamic vinegar

½ teaspoon salt

1 bunch green beans, trimmed

3 cups water

1 green bell pepper, chopped

1 avocado, chopped, pitted

Directions

In your Crock-pot add the water, red beans, chickpea, oil, and salt, stir well and let it cook for 6 hours on high.

Now add in the green beans and cook again for another hour.

Now put to a bowl and drain off the excessive water, let it cool.

Combine the chicken, green beans, and red beans with lemon juice, bell pepper, and avocado.

Season with pepper and drizzle vinegar. Serve and enjoy.

133. Crock-Pot Roasted Zucchini and Carrots

(Time: 240 minutes \ Servings: 6)

Ingredients

3 carrots, peeled, diced

2 zucchinis, sliced

1 cup tomato sauce

¼ teaspoon rosemary

¼ teaspoon black pepper

1 teaspoon vinegar

½ teaspoon salt

1 tablespoon oil

1 teaspoon mint leaves, chopped

Directions

In your Crock-pot add the carrots, zucchini, rosemary, salt, and pepper, tomato sauce, vinegar, and oil, stir well and let it cook for 4 hours on high.

Now transfer to a serving dish and sprinkle mint leaves as much you like. Serve and enjoy.

134. Feta Stuffed Bell Peppers

(Time: 240 minutes \ Servings: 3)

Ingredients

2-3 green bell peppers, cut from stem

1 cup feta cheese, crumbled

1 cup can tomatoes

1 onion, chopped

½ teaspoon black pepper

½ teaspoon salt

1 tablespoon lemon juice

1 tablespoon oil

Directions

In a bowl add the feta cheese, tomatoes, onion, salt, pepper, and lemon juice, mix well. Drizzle the bell peppers with oil and fill with 4-5 tablespoons of the feta mixture.

Place into a greased crock-pot and cover with a lid.

Let it cook for 4 hours on high. Serve and enjoy.

135. Baked Crock-Pot Cauliflower and Squash

(Time: 24- minutes \ Servings: 4)

Ingredients

1 cup cauliflower florets

1 cup squash, peeled, chunks

1 cup cherry tomatoes

¼ teaspoon black pepper

¼ cup chicken broth

1 red bell pepper, sliced

1 zucchini, sliced

½ teaspoon salt

Directions

In the Crock-pot add all the ingredients and cover up with a lid.

Cook for 4 hours on high. Serve and enjoy.

136. Spinach and Chickpea Stew

(Time: 420 minutes \ Servings: 4)

Ingredients

1 cup spinach, leaves

1 cup chickpea, soaked

¼ teaspoon black pepper

1 teaspoon vinegar

½ teaspoon salt

1 tablespoon oil

4 cups vegetable broth

Directions

In your Crock-pot add put all ingredients and toss.

Let it cook for 7 hours on high.

Then transfer to a serving dish.

Serve and enjoy.

137. Steam Tomatoes and Green Beans

(Time: 240 minutes \ Servings: 3)

Ingredients

1 bunch green beans, trimmed

2 oz. tomatoes, halved

1 teaspoon chili powder

3 tablespoons vinegar

½ teaspoon onion powder

½ teaspoon salt

Directions

In a baking dish the tomatoes, green beans, salt, chili powder, and mix well.

Add 2 cups of water into your Crock pot and place a baking dish into pot.

Cover the pot with a lid and let it cook for 4 hours on high.

Transfer to a serving dish. Serve and enjoy.

138. Steamed Broccoli and Carrots

(Time: 240 minutes \ Servings: 3)

Ingredients

3 cups broccoli florets

2 carrots, peeled, thinly sliced

1 teaspoon black pepper

1 tablespoon vinegar

½ teaspoon salt

Directions

In a baking dish add the broccoli, vinegar, carrots, salt, pepper, and toss well.

Add 2 cups of water into the Crock pot and place a baking dish into pot.

Cover the pot with a lid and cook for 4 hours on high.

Transfer to a serving dish.

Serve and enjoy.

139. White Beans and Carrot Adobo

(Time: 240 minutes \ Servings: 3)

Ingredients

1 cup white beans, soaked

3 carrots, peeled, diced

1 red bell pepper, sliced

1 onion, sliced

½ teaspoon garlic paste

¼ teaspoon ginger paste

1 teaspoon white pepper

2 tablespoons vinegar

½ teaspoon salt

1 teaspoon oil

2 cups vegetable broth

Directions

Transfer the white beans, water, ginger g paste, and salt into the Crock-pot and mix well.

Cover the pot with la id and let to cook for 3 hours on high.

Now add in the bell pepper, oil, carrots, onion, vinegar, and pepper.

Mix well and let it cook on high for 1 hour.

Transfer to a serving dish and enjoy.

140. Eggplant Pasta

(Time: 120 minutes \ Servings: 3)

Ingredients

2 medium eggplants, sliced

½ teaspoon chili powder

2 cup tomato sauce

1 garlic clove, minced

½ teaspoon salt

1 package pasta

2 cups chicken broth

1 teaspoon oil

Directions

In the Crock-pot add the pasta, salt, oil, and chicken broth, leave to cook on high for 1 hour.

Now add the egg plant, chili powder, tomato sauce and mix well.

Cook again for another hour on high temperature. Serve and enjoy.

141. Sweet and Sour Squash Delight

(Time: 120 minutes \ Servings: 4)

Ingredients

2 oz. squash, peeled chunks

½ cup brown sugar

2 tablespoon soya sauce

2 tablespoons vinegar

¼ cup walnuts, chopped

½ teaspoon oregano

1 teaspoon mint leaves, chopped

1 teaspoon white pepper

½ teaspoon salt

¼ cup orange juice

Directions

In the Crock-pot add the squash, brown sugar, vinegar, salt, pepper, oregano, orange juice, soya sauce and stir until well mixed

Cover the pot with a lid and let it cook for 2 hours on high T.

Transfer to a serving dish, sprinkle mint leave and walnuts.

142. Baked Squash Chips

(Time: 120 minutes \ Servings: 3)

Ingredients

2 oz. squash, cut into 1 inch slices

1 teaspoon black pepper

½ teaspoon salt

1 teaspoon oil

Directions

In the Crock-pot spread aluminum sheet and transfer squash slice.

Season with salt and pepper.

Drizzle oil and wrap into an aluminum foil by folding foil over squash slice.

Cover the pot with a lid and let it cook for 2 hours on high.

Serve and enjoy.

143. Potato Lasagne

(Time: 180 minutes \ Servings: 6)

Ingredients

5 large potatoes, cut into round slices

5-6 lasagna strips, boiled

1 teaspoon garlic paste

2 cups tomato sauce

2 tablespoons olive oil

1 cup mozzarella cheese, grated

½ cup cream cheese, crumbled

Directions

Grease the Crock-pot with oil. Spread 3-4 lasagna strips at the bottom and place 4-5 potato slices in a circular form.

Sprinkle some mozzarella cheese and pour 4-5 tablespoons of tomato sauce.

Place lasagna strips and all the remaining ingredients in the same way.

Top with mozzarella and cream cheese. Cover the pot with a lid and leave it cook for 3 hours. Serve and enjoy.

144. Hot Eggplant Bharta

(Time: 120 minutes \ Servings: 3)

Ingredients

3 large eggplants

2 tomatoes, chopped

¼ teaspoon turmeric powder

¼ teaspoon coriander powder

½ teaspoon chili powder

½ teaspoon salt

½ teaspoon garlic paste

2 tablespoons oil

¼ cup chicken broth

2 tablespoons butter

Directions

Brush the eggplant with oil and place directly on high flame till its skin becomes light gold color. Now peel off the skin and chop the eggplants.

Add butter into the Crock pot with the chopped eggplants, salt, tomatoes, garlic, chili powder, turmeric powder, coriander powder, chicken broth, mix and cook for 3 hours on high temperature or for 5 hours on low temperature.

Transfer to a serving dish and serve with bread or rice.

145. Cinnamon Flavoured Steamed Cabbage

(Time: 120 minutes \ Servings: 2)

Ingredients

1 medium cabbage, cut into 4 equal pieces

1 teaspoon white pepper

1 teaspoon cinnamon powder

2 tablespoon lemon juice

½ teaspoon salt

Directions

In a baking dish place the cabbage and season with salt, pepper, and cinnamon powder.

Add 2 cups of water in the Crock pot and place a baking dish into pot. Cover the pot with a lid and let it cook for 2 hours on high.Transfer to a serving dish and drizzle lemon juice.

146. Cabbage Rolls

(Time: 180 minutes \ Servings: 3)

Ingredients

3-4 cabbage leaves

2 cups tomato sauce

4 potatoes, boiled

1 tablespoon coriander, chopped

¼ cup feta cheese

½ teaspoon chili powder

½ teaspoon salt

½ teaspoon garlic paste

2 tablespoons oil

¼ cup chicken broth

2 tablespoons butter

Directions

In a saucepan add 1 cup water and let it boil. Add in the cabbage leaves and blanch for 1 minute. Remove from the water and place it aside.

Take a bowl and add the potatoes, feta cheese, salt, chili powder, coriander and mash with potato masher.

Now place 1 leave on clean surface and top with 4-5 tablespoons of the potato mixture, wrap it up in the form of a roll.

Now transfer the oil, garlic, and tomato sauce into the Crock-pot and place the cabbage rolls inside. Let it cook on low for 4 hours. Serve and enjoy.

147. Garlic Flavoured Kale

(Time: 120 minutes \ Servings: 3)

Ingredients

2 bunches of kale leaves

4-5 garlic cloves, minced

1 tablespoon coconut oil

¼ cup soya sauce

½ teaspoon salt

Directions

In the Crock-pot place aluminum foil and transfer the kale leaves with garlic, soya sauce, salt and oil, mix well.

Fold aluminum foil over the kale leaves and cook for 2 hours on high.Serve and enjoy.

148. Honey Flavoured Carrots

(Time: 180 minutes \ Servings: 4)

Ingredients

4 oz. carrot, peeled

½ cup honey

¼ teaspoon cinnamon powder

¼ cup soya sauce

½ teaspoon salt

Directions

In the Crock-Pot transfer all ingredients and cover with a lid.

Cook on high temperature for 3 hours.

Serve and enjoy.

149. Soya Lime Bok Choy

(Time: 120 minutes \ Servings: 3)

Ingredients

3 oz. Bok Choy

½ cup soya sauce

¼ cup oyster sauce

1 lime, thinly sliced

Directions

In the Crock-pot transfer all ingredients and toss well.

Let it cook for 2 hours on high.

Serve and enjoy.

150. Bok Choy Pancit

(Time: 360 minutes \ Servings: 3)

Ingredients

1 package rice noodles

3 cups chicken broth

1 eggplant, sliced

2 carrots, chopped

2 oz. Bok Choy, sliced

1 tablespoon oil

½ teaspoon salt

Directions

In the Crock-Pot add all ingredients and combine well.

Let it s cook for 6 hours on low.

Serve and enjoy.

Crock-Pot Soup Recipes

151. Chicken Tomato Soup

(Time: 240 minutes \ Servings: 4)

Ingredients

½ cup chicken, pieces, boneless

1 cup tomato sauce

2-3 garlic cloves, minced

2 tablespoon lemon juice

¼ teaspoon black pepper

½ teaspoon salt

½ cup sour cream, whipped

2 cups chicken broth

Few tortilla chips

2 tablespoon butter

Directions

Melt the butter into the Crock-pot and add the chicken stir for 1 minute.

Now add the tomato sauce, chicken broth, salt, pepper, garlic and mix well.

Let it cook on low temperature for 4 hours.

Ladle to a serving dish and drizzle lemon juice.

Top with tortilla chips and puddle of sour cream.

Enjoy.

152. Carrot Puree Soup

(Time: 180 minutes \ Servings: 4)

Ingredients

2 oz. carrots, peeled, chopped

2-3 garlic cloves, minced

1 onion, chopped

½ teaspoon black pepper

½ teaspoon salt

½ cup sour cream, whipped

2 cups chicken broth

Directions

In the Crock-pot add the carrots, garlic, onion, chicken broth, salt, and mix well.

Cook on low for 2h on high. Now add the cream, black pepper, and mix, let it cook for 1 hour. Transfer to a blender and blend until it becomes puree.

Ladle to a serving dish and serve.

153. Bok Choy Soup

(Time: 240 minutes \ Servings: 4)

Ingredients

3 oz. Bok Choy

1 inch ginger slice

2-3 garlic cloves, minced

¼ teaspoon white pepper

½ teaspoon salt

3 cups chicken broth

2 tablespoons soya sauce

Directions

Transfer all ingredients into the Crock-pot and mix well.

Let it cook and cover on low for 4 hours.

Serve and enjoy.

154. Chicken and Mushroom Soup

(Time: 180 minutes \ Servings: 4)

Ingredients

½ cup chicken, pieces, boneless

1 cup heavy cream

1 cup coconut milk

2-3 garlic cloves, minced

¼ teaspoon black pepper

½ teaspoon salt

1 cup mushrooms, sliced

1 cup chicken broth

2 tablespoon butter

Directions

In the Crock-pot add the chicken, butter, milk, cream, garlic, pepper, mushrooms, chicken broth, and salt, mix well and let it cook on low for 4 hours.

Ladle to a serving dish and serve.

155. Zucchini Soup

(Time: 240 minutes \ Servings: 4)

Ingredients

4-6 large zucchinis, chopped

3 cups vegetable broth

2-3 garlic cloves, minced

1 inch ginger slice

¼ teaspoon black pepper

½ teaspoon salt

1 tablespoon butter

Dircctions

In the Crock-pot add the zucchini, ginger, garlic, vegetable broth, pepper, and utter, stir and combine.

Let it cook on low for 4 hour.

Remove from the Crock-pot and let it cool for 2-3 minutes.

Pour to a blender and blend till puree. Serve and enjoy.

156. Chicken Avcado Soup

(Time: 180 minutes \ Servings: 4)

Ingredients

2 chicken breasts, cut into 2 inch pieces

2 tablespoons oyster sauce

2 carrots, finely chopped

1 avocado, pitted, chopped

¼ cup spring onion, chopped

2-3 garlic cloves, minced

½ teaspoon salt

3 cups chicken broth

¼ cup sour cream whipped

Directions

In the Crock-pot add the chicken, oyster sauce, carrots, salt, avocado, chicken broth, garlic, and stir and combine.

Cover up with a lid and cook on low for 4 hour.

Ladle to a serving dish and sprinkle spring onion and top with puddle of cream.

157. Orange and Chicken Shred Soup

(Time: 240 minutes \ Servings: 6)

Ingredients

2 chicken breasts

1 cup orange juice

¼ cup spring onion, chopped

2-3 garlic cloves, minced

2 tablespoon lemon juice

¼ teaspoon black pepper

½ teaspoon salt

3 cups chicken broth

1 onion, chopped

1 tablespoon oil

Directions

In a pan add the butter and sauce onion and garlic for 1 minute.

Transfer to your Crock pot with the chicken, orange juice, salt, pepper, and chicken broth, stir well. Cook on high temperature for 3 hour.

Now open the lid and shred the chicken with fork until lightly shredded.

Cook again for another hour. Ladle to a serving bowls and drizzle lemon juice.

Sprinkle spring onion and enjoy.

158. Squash Velvet Soup

(Time: 240 minutes \ Servings: 6)

Ingredients

1 cup squash, peeled, chunks

1 cup cream

2-3 garlic cloves, minced

½ teaspoon salt

3 cups vegetable broth

1 tablespoon butter

Directions

In the Crock-pot add all ingredients and mix well.

Cook on low for 5 hours.

Now remove from the pot and transfer to a blender.

Make it a puree.

Pour to serving bowls and serve immediately.

159. Strawberry and Tomato Soup

(Time: 180 minutes \ Servings: 4)

Ingredients

1 cup strawberries

½ cup tomato puree

1 cup vegetable broth

2 cups orange juice

2 tablespoon lemon juice

¼ teaspoon black pepper

½ teaspoon salt

1 teaspoon brown sugar

2tablespoon mint leaves, finely chopped

Directions

Put the strawberries, tomato puree, orange juice, vegetable broth, salt, sugar, and pepper inside the Crock-Pot. Cook on high for 3 hours.

Pour to a blender and blend until nicely smooth. Ladle to serving bowls and drizzle lemon juice. Sprinkle mint and serve.

160. Broccoli Cream Soup

(Time: 240 minutes \ Servings: 6)

Ingredients

2 cups broccoli florets

1 carrot, finely chopped

2-3 garlic cloves, minced

¼ teaspoon white pepper

1 can chicken soup

½ teaspoon salt

½ cup sour cream, whipped

2 cups chicken broth

Directions

Transfer all ingredients into the Crock-pot and cover up with a lid.

Cook on low for 4 hours. Now pour to a blender and blend for about 20-30 seconds.

Ladle to a serving bowls and serve.

161. Pear and Apple Soup

(Time: 120 minutes \ Servings: 3)

Ingredients

4 apples, peeled, chopped

3-4 peas, chopped

1 bananas

1 cup coconut milk
1 teaspoon vinegar

¼ teaspoon black pepper

¼ teaspoon salt

¼ cup brown sugar

2 cups chicken broth

Directions

In a blender add the apples, milk, pear, banana, pepper, salt, chicken broth, vinegar, and sugar.
Blend until puree.

Pour inside the Crock-pot and let it cook for 2 hours on high.

Ladle to serving bowls. Serve and enjoy.

162. Chicken Spinach Soup

(Time: 240 minutes \ Servings: 6)

Ingredients

1 cup spinach leave

2 potatoes, peeled, diced

2 carrots, peeled, sliced

1 oz. chicken, pieces

2 tablespoon soya sauce

2 tablespoons oyster sauce

2-3 garlic cloves, minced

2 tablespoon lemon juice

¼ teaspoon black pepper

½ teaspoon salt

3 cups chicken broth

Directions

In the Crock-pot add all ingredients and stir well. Cook on low for 4 hours. Pour to serving bowls. Serve hot and enjoy.

163. Cooling Strawberry Soup

(Time: 240 minutes \ Servings: 3)

Ingredients

2 cups strawberries, chopped

¼ cup sugar

2 cups pineapple juice

1 cup coconut milk

1 tablespoon lemon juice

Directions

Put all ingredients into the Crock-pot and mix well.

Let it cook on high for 4 hours.

Pour to a blender and blend till puree.

Ladle to serving bowls and serve.

164. Hot Miso Soup

(Time: 120 minutes \ Servings: 4)

Ingredients

2 tablespoons miso paste

½ cup chicken, small pieces

1 cup tomato sauce

2-3 garlic cloves, minced

2 tablespoon lemon juice

¼ teaspoon black pepper

½ teaspoon salt

3 cups chicken broth

1tablespoon spring onion, chopped

Directions

Put all ingredients into the Crock-pot and mix well.

Let it cook on low for 2 hours.

Pour to serving dish and serve.

165. Split Gram Soup

(Time: 240 minutes \ Servings: 2)

Ingredients

2 cups split gram, soaked

¼ teaspoon turmeric powder

2-3 garlic cloves, minced

1 inch ginger slice

¼ teaspoon white pepper

2 tablespoon brown sugar

1 teaspoon soya sauce

½ teaspoon salt

½ cup chicken soup

3 cups chicken broth

Directions

Put all ingredients into the Crock-pot and mix well.

Let it cook on high for 4 hours.

Now transfer to a blender and blend till puree. Pour to a serving bowl and serve.

166. Sweet Potato Soup

(Time: 180 minutes \ Servings: 4)

Ingredients

3 oz. sweet potatoes, peeled, sliced

½ cup brown sugar

1 cup pineapple juice

¼ teaspoon black pepper

½ teaspoon salt

2 cups chicken broth

Directions

Transfer all ingredients into the Crock-pot and mix well.

Cook on low temperature for 4 hours.

Now transfer the soup to a blender and blend till creamy.

Pour to a serving dish and serve.

167. Mixed Vegetable Soup with Chickpeas

(Time: 300 minutes \ Servings: 5)

Ingredients

3 oz. potatoes, sliced

3 carrots, peeled, sliced

2 sweet potatoes, peeled, sliced

2 zucchinis, sliced

2 cups chickpea, soaked

¼ cup ginger juice

¼ teaspoon white pepper

½ teaspoon salt

4 cups chicken broth

Directions

In the Crock-pot add the chickpea, chicken broth, salt and pepper, mix well.

Cook on low for 3 hours. Now add the potatoes, sweet potatoes, ginger juice, white pepper, carrots, and zucchini.

Cover and cook on high for 2 hours. Pour to a serving bowl and serve.

168. Asparagus Cream Soup

(Time: 180 minutes \ Servings: 3)

Ingredients

2 oz. asparagus shoots

¼ teaspoon black pepper

½ teaspoon salt

2 tablespoon sugar

1 cup sour cream

½ cup coconut milk

Directions

Transfer all ingredients in the Crock-pot and mix well.

Cook on high for 3 hours.

Transfer to a blender and blend till creamy.

Pour to a serving dish and serve.

169. Tomato Soya Chili Soup

(Time: 180 minutes \ Servings: 3)

Ingredients

2 can tomatoes

¼ cup soya sauce

1 teaspoon thyme

1 red bell pepper, chopped

¼ teaspoon chili pepper

½ teaspoon salt

2 tablespoon sugar

2 cups chicken broth

1 garlic clove, minced

Directions

Transfer all ingredients into the Crock-pot and mix well.

Let it cook on high for 3 hours.

Transfer to a blender and blend till creamy. Pour to a serving bowl and serve.

170. Sausage and Red Beans Soup

(Time: 420 minutes \ Servings: 4)

Ingredients

4 oz. sausage, cut into slices

1 onion, chopped

2 leak shoots, trimmed

¼ teaspoon black pepper

½ teaspoon salt

2 cups vegetable broth

1 tablespoon vinegar

1 tablespoon soya sauce

2-3 garlic cloves, minced

1 inch ginger slice, chopped

Directions

Transfer all the ingredients into the Crock-pot and mix well.

Let it cook on high for 7 hours.

Pour to a serving dish and serve.

171. Red Lentil Puree Soup

(Time: 240 minutes \ Servings: 3)

Ingredients

1 cup red lentil, soaked

2 carrots, peeled, chopped

¼ teaspoon black pepper

¼ teaspoon chili powder

¼ teaspoon cinnamon powder

½ teaspoon salt

2 cups chicken broth

Directions

Transfer all ingredients into the crock-pot and mix well.

Let it cook on high for 4 hours.

Transfer to a blender and blend until creamy. Pour to a serving dish and serve.

172. Creamy Peas Soup

(Time: 240 minutes \ Servings: 4)

Ingredients

3 cups peas

3 cups water

¼ teaspoon white pepper

1 inch ginger slice

½ teaspoon salt

1 cup sour cream

½ cup cream cheese

Directions

In the Crock-pot add the peas, water, salt and cook on high temperature for 6 hours.

Now add the sour cream, cream cheese, ginger, pepper and mix well.

Cook on high for 1 hour.

Transfer to a blender and blend till creamy.

Pour to a serving dish and serve.

173. Sweet Potato Ginger Soup

(Time: 180 minutes \ Servings: 3)

Ingredients

2 oz. sweet potatoes, peeled, diced

2 tablespoon honey

½ cup sugar

1 cup sour cream

½ cup coconut milk

½ cup boiled and peeled almonds

Directions

Transfer all ingredients in the Crock-pot and mix well. Cook on high for 3 hours.

Transfer to a blender and blend till creamy. Pour to a serving dish and top with almonds.

Serve and enjoy.

174. Semolina Milk Delight Soup

(Time: 180 minutes \ Servings: 4)

Ingredients

1 cup semolina, soaked for 10 minutes

½ teaspoon aniseeds

½ teaspoon green cardamom powder

1 cup milk

1 cup chicken cream

1 pinch salt

½ cup sugar

1 cup almond milk

Directions

Transfer all ingredients into the Crock-pot and mix well.

Cook on high for 3 hours.

Pour to a serving dish and serve.

Enjoy.

175. Coconut and Carrot Soup

(Time: 240 minutes \ Servings: 4)

Ingredients

2 oz. carrots, peeled, chopped

2 tablespoon sugar

4 tablespoons honey

¼ cup sour cream

½ cup orange juice

1 inch ginger slice

2 cup coconut milk

Directions

Transfer all ingredients into the Crock-pot and mix well.

Let it cook on high for 3 hours.

Transfer to a blender and blend till creamy. Pour to a serving dish and serve. Enjoy.

Crock-Pot Dessert Recipes

176. Soothing Peach Crumble

(Time: 120 minutes \ Servings: 3)

Ingredients

3 cup peaches, seeded, sliced

1 cup pineapple juice

¼ cup sugar

3 tablespoon honey

1 cup whipped cream

1 cup mango juice

Directions

In the Crock Pot add the mango juice, pineapple juice, sugar, peach slices and combine.
Cook on low for 2 hours. Transfer to a serving dish and drizzle honey.
Top with a puddle of whipped cream. Enjoy.

177. Chocolate Rich Mocha Cake

(Time: 120 minutes \ Servings: 6)

Ingredients

1 cup all-purpose flour

1 cup cocoa powder

½ cup caster sugar

¼ cup raw chocolate, melted

1 teaspoon baking powder

1 pinch baking soda

1 pinch salt

½ cup milk

2 eggs, whisked

4 tablespoons butter, melted

Directions

In a bowl add the butter, sugar and egg, beat for 1-2 minutes.

Add in the baking powder, baking soda, chocolate, salt, sugar, cocoa powder, flour and milk, whisked for 1-2 minutes.

Spread aluminum foil into the Crock pot in the form of round cup.

Transfer the mixture into this cup and cover up the pot with a lid. Cook for 2-3 hours on high. Transfer to a platter and dust some caster sugar on top. Serve and enjoy.

178. Blueberry Cobbler

(Time: 120 minutes \ Servings: 4)

Ingredients

1 can pie filling

2 cup blackberries

½ cup all-purpose flour

½ cup caster sugar

1 pinch baking soda

½ cup milk

2 eggs, whisked

Directions

In a bowl add the milk, pie filling, flour, sugar and eggs, mix well. Pour into a greased Crock pot and top with blueberries. Cook for 2 hours on high. Transfer to a serving dish and enjoy.

179. Pineapple Pie Crumble

(Time: 120 minutes \ Servings: 3)

Ingredients

1 cup pineapple chunks

½ cup pineapple juice

1 cup all-purpose flour

2 tablespoons butter, melted

½ cup caster sugar

1 pinch baking soda

½ cup milk

2 eggs, whisked

Directions

In a bowl add milk, pineapple chunks, butter, pineapple juice, flour, sugar and eggs, mix well. Pour into a greased crockpot and cover with a lid.

Cook for 2 hours on high. Transfer to a serving dish.

180. Strawberry Cobbler

(Time: 120 minutes \ Servings: 3)

Ingredients

1 cup strawberries, chunks

1 cup all-purpose flour

1 teaspoon baking powder

½ teaspoon vanilla extract

2 tablespoons butter, melted

½ cup caster sugar

1 pinch baking soda

1 cup milk

2 eggs, whisked

1 cup cream, whipped

Directions

In a bowl add milk, strawberries, butter, baking powder, vanilla extract, flour, sugar and eggs, mix well. Pour into a greased crockpot and cover with a lid.

Let it cook for 2 hours on high. Transfer to a serving dish and top with whipped cream.

Serve and enjoy.

181. Chocolate Silk Bowl

(Time: 120 minutes \ Servings: 3)

Ingredients

1 cup raw chocolate

1 cup all-purpose flour

4 tablespoons butter, melted

½ cup caster sugar

½ cup cocoa powder

1 pinch baking soda

1 cup milk

2 eggs, whisked

1 cup whipped cream

Directions

In a bowl add the milk, chocolate, butter, baking soda, cocoa powder, cocoa powder, flour, sugar and eggs, mix well.

Pour into a greased Crock pot and cover with a lid. Cook for 2 hours on high temperature.

Place to a serving dish and top with whipped cream. Serve and enjoy.

182. Dumb Cake

(Time: 120 minutes \ Servings: 3)

Ingredients

1 cup apple pie mix

1 cup all-purpose flour

4 tablespoon cocoa powder

3 tablespoons butter, melted

½ cup caster sugar

1 pinch baking soda

½ cup milk

1 egg, whisked

Directions

In a bowl add the cocoa powder, butter, baking soda, milk, apple pie mix, flour, sugar and egg, mix thoroughly. Pour into a greased Crock pot and cover it up.

Cook for 2 hours on high. Place into a serving dish and enjoy.

183. Chocolate Covered Peanuts

(Time: 120 minutes \ Servings: 6)

Ingredients

6 oz. dark chocolate chips

2 oz. white chocolate

¼ cup sugar syrup

2 tablespoons butter, melted

2 cups peanuts

Directions

In the Crock-pot add the white chocolate, dark chocolate chips, sugar syrup, butter, and peanuts, combine well and cover with a lid.

Cook for 2 hours on high.

Transfer to a dish and leave to cool down.

Cut into chunks and serve or preserve into an air tight jar.

Serve and enjoy.

184. Chocolate Pudding

(Time: 120 minutes \ Servings: 4)

Ingredients

1 cup chocolate chips

4 cups milk

½ cup almond, hopped

2 cups cocoa powder

2 cup all-purpose flour

3 tablespoons butter, melted

½ cup caster sugar

2 eggs, beaten

Directions

Take a bowl and add in the chocolate chips, almonds, milk, butter, cocoa powder, flour, sugar and eggs, mix well. Pour into a greased Crock pot, cover with a lid.

Cook for 2 hours on high. Transfer to a serving dish and enjoy.

185. Rice and Chocolate Pudding

(Time: 120 minutes \ Servings: 3)

Ingredients

1 cup rice, soaked

1 cup raw chocolate

2 cups coconut milk

½ teaspoon green cardamom powder

5 tablespoons butter, melted

½ cup caster sugar

½ cup cocoa powder

2 cups milk

Directions

In a Crock-pot add all ingredients, then toss and combine.

Let it cook for 2 hours on high.

Transfer to a serving dish.

Serve and enjoy.

186. Chocolate Chia Pudding

(Time: 120 minutes \ Servings: 3)

Ingredients

1 cup chia seeds

2 cups raw chocolate

½ cup dates, chopped

4 tablespoons butter, melted

½ cup caster sugar

½ cup cocoa powder

2 cups milk

Directions

In a Crock-pot add all ingredients and mix them up well.

Cook for 2 hours on high. Place into a serving dish and enjoy.

187. Banana Oatmeal

(Time: 240 minutes \ Servings: 3)

Ingredients

1 cup oats

3 bananas, peeled, chopped

½ cup blackberries

½ cup brown sugar

½ teaspoon green cardamom powder

4 tablespoons butter, melted

½ cup caster sugar

3 cups milk

Directions

In a Crock-pot add all the ingredients; toss and combine.

Cook for 2 hours on high.

Place into a serving dish.

Serve and enjoy.

188. Carrot Cake

(Time: 120 minutes \ Servings: 3)

Ingredients

1 cup carrots, shredded

1 cup all-purpose flour

½ teaspoon baking powder

2 tablespoon yogurt

3 tablespoons butter, melted

½ cup caster sugar

3 eggs, whisked

2 cups milk

1 cup cream

½ cup sugar syrup

Directions

In a bowl add the eggs, sugar, butter and beat for 1-2 minutes.

Now add the baking powder, milk, yogurt, flour and mix thoroughly. Cook for 2 hours on high. Then whisk cream with sugar syrup and mix.

Transfer to a serving dish and top with whipped cream. Serve and enjoy.

189. Apple Pie Crumble

(Time: 120 minutes \ Servings: 3)

Ingredients

6 large apples, peeled, thinly sliced

1 cup all-purpose flour

4 tablespoon butter, melted

½ cup caster sugar

3 eggs, whisked

2 cups milk

1 tablespoon lemon juice

Directions

In a Crock-pot place all apple slices and drizzle lemon juice.

In a bowl add the eggs, milk, flour, sugar, butter and mix well.

Pour over apple mixture and cover up with a lid.

Cook for 2 hours on high. Transfer to a serving dish and enjoy.

190. Carrot Pudding

(Time: 120 minutes \ Servings: 3)

Ingredients

4 carrots, shredded

1 cup sour cream

¼ teaspoon chili powder

½ teaspoon green cardamom powder

1 cup condense milk

¼ cup caster sugar

2 cups milk

Directions

In a Crock-pot add the carrots, green cardamom powder, milk, sugar, condense milk and mix well. Cook for 2 hours on high temperature.

Transfer to a serving dish and top with sour cream. Sprinkle chili powder. Serve and enjoy.

191. Sweet Dates Crunches

(Time: 60 minutes \ Servings: 3)

Ingredients

1 cup dates

½ cup pistachios

½ cup peanuts

½ teaspoon green cardamom powder

3 tablespoons butter, melted

½ cup brown sugar

½ teaspoon cocoa powder

2 cups milk

Dircctions

In a Crock-pot add all ingredients, mix well

Let it cook for 2 hours on high.

Transfer to a serving dish and enjoy.

192. Crock-Pot Strawberry Sauce

(Time: 60 minutes \ Servings: 3)

Ingredients

1 cup strawberries
½ cup pineapple juice

½ cup caster sugar
2 tablespoon lime juice

Directions

In the Crock-pot add all ingredients, mix well. Let it cook for 1 hour on high.

Pour to a blender and blend till puree. Serve and enjoy.

193. Baked Apples and Chickpea Chat

(Time: 420 minutes \ Servings: 4)

Ingredients

1 cup chickpea, soaked
1 cranberry sauce
¼ cup soya sauce

4 apples, chopped
½ cup brown sugar
1 cup water

Directions

In a Crock-pot add the chickpea with water and cook on low for 6 hours.

Then add the soya sauce, apples, cranberry sauce, sugar and mix well.

Cook for another hour on high temperature. Serve and enjoy.

194. Baked Apples

(Time: 120 minutes \ Servings: 3)

Ingredients

2 large apples
3 tablespoon butter, melted

½ cup sugar
1 cup pineapple juice

Directions

Brush the apples with butter. In the Crock pot add the sugar and the pineapple juice, mix well.
Put the apples inside the pot and cook for 2 hours on high. Transfer to a serving dish.

195. Cinnamon Glazed Apples

(Time: 60 minutes \ Servings: 3)

Ingredients

5-6 large apples, peeled, sliced

1 cup maple syrup

1 tablespoon lime juice

¼ teaspoon cinnamon powder

Directions

Place apple slices into the Crock-pot and pour maple syrup. Sprinkle cinnamon powder. Let it cook for 1 hour on high. Transfer to a serving dish and enjoy.

196. Banana and Chocolate Dessert

(Time: 60 minutes \ Servings: 3)

Ingredients

4 ripe bananas, peeled

1 cup raw chocolate

5 tablespoons butter, melted

½ cup caster sugar

½ cup cocoa powder

2 cups milk

Directions

In a bowl add bananas and mash with fork.

In a Crock-pot add the bananas, milk, chocolate, butter, cocoa powder, and sugar, toss and combine. Cook for 1 hour on high. Transfer to a serving dish and enjoy.

197. Moist Bread Pudding

(Time: 60 minutes \ Servings: 5)

Ingredients

2 oz. bread, crumbled

4 eggs, whisked

¼ teaspoon vanilla extract

5 tablespoons butter, melted

½ cup sugar syrup

4 cups milk

Directions

Transfer the bread pieces into the Crockpot, pour the milk, butter, sugar syrup, vanilla extract, eggs and cover with a lid.

Cook for 1 hour on high temperature. Transfer to a serving dish and enjoy.

198. Chocolate Fudge

(Time: 60 minutes \ Servings: 6)

Ingredients

1 cup dark chocolate

1 cup white chocolate

½ cup chocolate chips

1 cup cashews, chopped

½ cup raising

2 cup milk

1 cup raw chocolate

2 tablespoons butter, melted

2 tablespoon sugar syrup

Directions

In a Crock-pot add the chocolate chips, white chocolate, dark chocolate, sugar syrup, butter, raising, cashews and mix them up well..

Cover and let it cook for 1 hour on high.

Transfer to a baking dish and let to sit for 1-2 hour at room temperature. Now cut into slices. Serve and enjoy.

199. Candied Loaded Pecan

(Time: 60 minutes \ Servings: 6)

Ingredients

2 cups pecans

¼ teaspoon vanilla extract

½ cup brown sugar

2 eggs, whisked

2 tablespoon milk

2 tablespoons butter, melted

Directions

In a Crock-pot put pecans and spread well.

In a medium bowl add the vanilla extract, butter, milk, eggs, and sugar whisk until the sugar is dissolved.

Pour over the pecans.

Cook for 1 hour on high temperature.

Transfer to a serving dish and enjoy.

200. Pumpkin Pudding

(Time: 120 minutes \ Servings: 3)

Ingredients

1 cup pumpkin puree

1 teaspoon pumpkin pie spice

1 cup cream, whisked

2 cups milk

½ teaspoon green cardamom powder

2 tablespoons butter, melted

½ cup caster sugar

½ cup all-purpose flour

1 egg, whisked

Directions

In a Crock-pot add the pumpkin puree, milk, sugar, flour, egg, butter and mix well.

Let it cook for 2 hours on high.

Transfer to a serving dish and top with whipped cream.

Serve and enjoy.

Thank you very much for reading this amazing book. We hope this book served you to cook delicious, easy and healthy meals, that are as well enjoyable.

Download the PDF version of this book with images of all recipes, here:

goo.gl/iYF2fP

Printed in Great Britain
by Amazon